The Writer's Companion

A Guide to First-Year Writing

with Excerpts from Writing Analytically

Second Edition

Kristin Ferebee | Edgar Singleton | Mike Bierschenk

CENGAGE
Learning·

Australia • Brazil • Japan • Korea • Mexico • Singapore • Spain • United Kingdom • United States

CENGAGE
Learning·

The Writer's Companion: A Guide to First-Year Writing, with Excerpts from Writing Analytically, Second Edition

Writing Analytically, 7th Edition
David Rosenwasser,Jill Stephen

© 2012, 2009, 2006 Cengage Learning, All rights reserved.

For product information and technology assistance, contact us at
Cengage Learning Customer & Sales Support, 1-800-354-9706

For permission to use material from this text or product,
submit all requests online at **cengage.com/permissions**
Further permissions questions can be emailed to
permissionrequest@cengage.com

This book contains select works from existing Cengage Learning resources and was produced by Cengage Learning Custom Solutions for collegiate use. As such, those adopting and/or contributing to this work are responsible for editorial content accuracy, continuity and completeness.

Compilation © 2016 Cengage Learning.

ISBN: 9781337691772

Cengage Learning
20 Channel Center Street
Boston, MA 02210
USA

Cengage Learning is a leading provider of customized learning solutions with office locations around the globe, including Singapore, the United Kingdom, Australia, Mexico, Brazil, and Japan. Locate your local office at:
www.international.cengage.com/region.
Cengage Learning products are represented in Canada by Nelson Education, Ltd.

For your lifelong learning solutions, visit **www.cengage.com/custom.**

Visit our corporate website at **www.cengage.com.**

BRIEF CONTENTS

CONTENTS

CHAPTER 4: The Art of Analysis

CHAPTER 6: Writing the Paper 65

CHAPTER 7: The Thesis Statement 87

CHAPTER 8: Using Images to Make Meaning   109

CHAPTER 9: What is a Paper Supposed to Look Like?   115

APPENDIX 1: Grammar and Punctuation   127

APPENDIX 2: Style Guide 143

INDEX 151

A NOTE FROM THE AUTHORS

Welcome to English 1110 and to the second edition of *The Writer's Companion: A Guide to First-Year Writing with Excerpts from Writing Analytically*. In addition to readings provided by your instructor, this text will provide you with an introduction to successful writing at the university level. Each chapter focuses on a particular aspect of writing that college faculty, writing instructors, and students themselves know to be central to achieving that goal. Our purpose in writing this book was to create a text tailored to your experience in English 1110 at Ohio State, and over the semester, you will likely read every word of *The Writer's Companion*. This book will allow you to explore concepts of analysis and writing style while incorporating the intellectual property of others into your writing effectively and ethically. You will find plenty of examples to work with, including sample sentences intended to delight as they help you polish your writing craft.

The First-Year Writing Program at Ohio State has long held to the idea that *analysis* is the most important intellectual work you will do at the university. This book, including the elements specific to English 1110 and the materials from David Rosenwasser and Jill Stephens' *Writing Analytically*, is designed to provide you with the tools for performing analysis at a sophisticated level. We are grateful to the authors of *Writing Analytically*, whose ideas have shaped the content of English composition at Ohio State over the years. We also express thanks to the hundreds of instructors and thousands of students in English 1110, whose feedback and contributions have shaped the course you will experience this semester. In particular, we wish to acknowledge graduate writing program administrators Pritha Prasad, Micah Rickerson, Sherita V. Roundtree, and Michael Shirzadian for their generous and thoughtful editorial input .

Best wishes for a great experience in English 1110. Remember that the authors of this book look forward to hearing from you as we consider ways of making it even more useful for future Ohio State writers.

Happy writing!

Kristin Ferebee
Edgar Singleton
Mike Bierschenk

CHAPTER 1

English 1110

For many students, "English class" has previously meant a class in which they read literature and wrote essays about its themes and symbolism. For some, it may have meant a class in which they learned English vocabulary and grammar. For most, it will have meant preparing for exams that evaluated students on their understanding of English rules and conventions—exams for which the correct answer was often chosen from (A), (B), (C), or (D).

These past experiences have formed valuable parts of your English education. However, they may have given you the impression that an English class is always primarily about literature, language, or memorization. In other words, you may have expected, when you signed up for English 1110, that you were entering a class in which most of your time would be spent reading books, diagramming sentences, or learning vocabulary—a class in which, once again, you would be asked to take tests where the correct answer was (A), (B), (C), or (D).

It may surprise you to learn that English 1110 is a different kind of class: you won't be memorizing a certain set of facts, and often, there won't be right or wrong answers to questions. Instead, English 1110 is a class about questions and answers themselves: how to ask effective questions, how to investigate possible answers to questions, how to compose reasonable answers to questions, and how to communicate these answers in the most effective way.

In the writing classroom, we even ask questions about the language we use to read and write. Most scholars in writing studies now agree that the teaching of writing should not only emphasize standard academic English (such as that found in academic articles, news magazines, and textbooks), but should also expose students to different *varieties* of English and the ways they function in society. In other words, the writing classroom should treat standard academic English not as a universal, "correct," or even ideal form of writing, but rather as simply one of many writing *varieties*, each of which has its own use and value depending on context. Of course, in reality, most of us already practice this kind of awareness in our social lives. It is unlikely, for instance, that you communicate with your college professor in the same way that you communicate with your best friend or roommate. At the same time, you probably know people who speak a different kind of English than you do. All of these varieties are appropriate and valuable in different contexts; when you switch your way of speaking from context to context, you are making deliberate and meaningful choices about your words, tone, and purpose.

English 1110 will teach you how to write in accordance to certain formal conventions of college writing, but it will not be a course on *how* to write a singular, universal, and grammatically "correct" English. Instead, the course will emphasize the higher-order concerns of standard academic writing such as critical analysis, logical and coherent argumentation, well-documented research, and appropriate style. Perhaps more importantly, it will also encourage you to think critically about the implications of your unique choices as a writer.

What are the Goals of English 1110?

The central goal of English 1110 is to transform its students into more sophisticated readers and writers. To this end, you will improve your ability to read and write both academic and public texts. You will learn to analyze the choices that authors have made, understand the reasons for and the effects of these choices, and then—as a writer yourself—make your own choices in order to create a clear and persuasive argument.

Of course, when we talk about writing in English 1110, we're really talking about a particular form of writing, sometimes called 'academic discourse', specifically the kind of academic writing that is used in the humanities. This differs from the styles and formats used in other disciplines such as the sciences, business, and medicine, not to mention the many different ways we write and speak in the world at large. All these different situations require their own ways of writing. That's not to say, however, that the writing you'll learn to do in this course won't prepare you to write in other classes and fields: far from it. No matter the field, writing in the university requires clarity, objectivity, well-supported claims, and ability to approach topics with an open mind. In English 1110, we accomplish these goals through analysis of texts.

In English 1110, a "text" that you read might not always involve printed words. A text might be an image, a video, or a song. All of these are objects that you can "read" in the same way that you read words, figuring out the meaning of them. At the same time, you may find yourself looking at word-based texts in new ways: instead of asking what a sentence is saying, you might ask, "How is this sentence saying what it's saying?" For instance, you might ask why a particular poem rhymes, or how the lyrics of a song paint a certain picture in your head.

Many of the strategies you will learn in English 1110 for reading and writing involve learning to carefully think about your own thinking. In other words: you will learn to examine your assumptions, ask yourself important questions, and challenge yourself to expand your mindset. This process is often called *metacognition*, a word that means "thinking about thinking." Metacognition helps students become better readers and writers—readers and writers who are confident in their ability to understand the various tools involved in the act of communication.

There are two particular toolkits that English 1110 will teach you to use. One of these is a set of tools that you will use to analyze texts. These tools will help you to break down texts, see them more clearly, and make connections between observations and ideas that help you to understand those texts. In English 1110, you will spend a great deal of time learning how to use these tools.

At the same time, you will learn to use the second toolkit: the rules and conventions of academic writing, which will allow you to write in a way that other people will find clear, logical, coherent, and persuasive. This set of tools includes not only conventions of grammar and syntax, but also stylistic conventions such as precise word choice, appropriate citation, and the skillful use of well-researched sources.

What Work will I do in English 1110?

The Analytical Research Project

The Analytical Research Project is a five-step process that will occupy most of your time, energy, and thought throughout the semester. Collectively, the steps of this project constitute 50% of your final course grade.

The final goal of the Analytical Research Project is to produce a clearly written, well-organized, complex, polished piece of academic writing, seven to eight pages in length. The analytical and research techniques that you learn and practice in the classroom during the semester will be vital in helping you complete these steps.

For the purpose of the Analytical Research Project, you won't start out with a topic. Instead, you will choose one **primary source**. The word *primary* comes from the word *primus*, meaning *first*: your primary source is the *first* thing you start with, and the *first* place you will look for information and ideas.

What is a Primary Source?   In English 1110, a primary source is a short text that is related to the course theme. Remember that, perhaps surprisingly, a "text" is not necessarily something made up of printed words. A primary source might be a poem or an excerpt from a novel, but it might also be a TV or magazine advertisement, a movie trailer, a music video, or even a song. It might be a scene from a film, or the cover of a comic book. It should be short enough that you can discuss every detail of it within 7-8 pages, yet substantial enough that it contains a wealth of details to discuss; it may be a small piece of a larger whole, but it should communicate a complete message.

For instance:

A strong primary source might be the poster for a summer blockbuster movie, a cell phone commercial, the lyrics to a pop song, or a SuperBowl ad. All of these texts can be understood by themselves and each has a definite purpose (though what that purpose *is* can be a little harder to pin down, which you'll learn about in chapter 3). They are also complex enough to warrant investigation without being so long that you can't wrap your head around them in 7–8 pages.

A less effective primary source might be the illustration for a news or magazine article (which doesn't make sense without the article it accompanies), a single frame from an anime (which is too short), a comic book (which is too long), a two-hour film (which is *way* too long), or a novel (which is *way*, way too long).

Primary source vs. **primary documents or primary artifacts**. You may have heard another definition of 'primary source', especially if you've done some kind of historical research. When looking at historical events and situations, researchers often prize texts produced by people involved in those events or situations—letters, treaties, graffiti, recorded interviews, etc.—because they give a direct view into the events as they occurred. These documents are sometimes referred to as primary documents or, confusingly, primary sources.

While these historical records can potentially make useful primary sources for the Analytical Research Project, depending on your class's theme, most primary sources in English 1110 aren't historical artifacts. But it's good to know this other, related term, which you may encounter in other classes.

Your primary source will be the central focus of your Analytical Research Project. You will spend most of the semester thinking about it—investigating it, asking questions about it, and engaging in research that will help you to construct an argument about it. Your primary source will be the engine that drives all five steps of this project.

As you move through the project, you will also learn to locate, read, and effectively integrate **secondary sources**.

What are Secondary Sources? Secondary sources are your *second* source of ideas and information. You will use them to inform, question, and shape your thoughts about your primary source. Secondary sources are written texts—such as academic papers, magazine or newspaper articles, essays, or chapters from books—that examine objects, data, or phenomena and make analytical claims about them. In other words, the work a secondary source does is very similar to the work that you will be doing when you analyze your primary source.

You might think of secondary sources as making up a large, ongoing conversation—a community of people engaged in analyzing the world. Your goal in the Analytical Research Project is to join that conversation. In order to do this, you will not only need to examine your primary source, but also consider and respond to arguments that other analysts have made. Later steps of the Analytical Research Project will focus on using secondary sources in a way that allows you to effectively engage in this kind of conversation.

The five steps of the Analytical Research Project are:

Step 1: Primary Source Analysis This step asks you to make careful observations about your primary source and to begin to develop these observations into analytical claims. You will also begin asking questions about your observations that will guide your future research. To do so, you will produce 2-3 pages of focused, meaningful analysis of your primary source.

Step 2: Annotated Bibliography This step asks you to read and evaluate 3-4 potential secondary sources. You will demonstrate that you have understood the arguments that these secondary sources make, and that you have considered how you might converse with these arguments in a way that expands your analysis of your primary source. You will also demonstrate your understanding of proper MLA Works Cited format.

Step 3: Secondary Source Integration This step asks you to revisit your work in the Primary Source Analysis, considering how the secondary sources you have read allow you to question, strengthen, re-shape, or extend the observations and claims you made in that assignment. You will expand and revise your analytical claims, integrating two secondary sources in order to produce 4-5 pages of thoughtful and coherent analysis. Your use of secondary sources should be meaningful and stylistically appropriate, demonstrating both a strong grasp of strategies for paraphrase or quotation and the ability to engage with the arguments of sources, rather than simply citing them as agreement or support.

Step 4: The Research Conference This step asks you to carefully consider your work on the Analytical Research Project, and to determine clear, organized, and realistic goals for the final stage of your work. You will do so by meeting with your teacher outside of class in order to discuss your plans. The Research Conference is an opportunity for you to receive personal guidance and specific suggestions from your teacher—guidance and suggestions that will help you build on your strengths and address your struggles as a student in order to create a strong final research paper.

Step 5: The Analytical Research Paper This final step asks you to demonstrate a clear and full grasp of all the skills you have learned over the course of the project, including the ability to perform thoughtful analysis, to integrate and cite secondary sources, and to construct a formally strong, thorough, coherent, and meaningful argument about your primary source.

You will polish, revise, and expand on the work of the Primary Source Analysis and the Secondary Source Integration in order to complete the 7-8 pages of your Analytical Research Paper, with correct MLA citations of sources and stylistically appropriate grammar and word choices.

The Symposium

The Symposium is an event that takes place over two weeks of English 1110, for which each student prepares a roughly 5-minute digital multimedia presentation on a topic that is relevant to the course theme. The Symposium Presentation is a sequence of 15 slides that you will design, create, and narrate for a public audience of your peers.

The word *symposium* comes from a Greek word that means *drinking party*. Greek drinking parties, however, were not very similar to the kinds of parties that you might be familiar with! They were opportunities for Greek citizens to give speeches, present new ideas, and debate important political and intellectual issues of the day. Over time, *symposium* has come to refer to a gathering that people attend in order to share new ideas and engage in this kind of debate.

The English 1110 Symposium is intended to be a place and time where you and your classmates can exchange and freely discuss the ideas that you have been investigating over the course of the semester. Because the Symposium occurs toward the end of the semester, you will have completed a great deal of research for the Analytical Research Project and will have developed new abilities to analyze texts and pursue arguments. The Symposium is an opportunity for you to use these abilities in a public setting.

The digital multimedia nature of your presentation also means that the Symposium allows you to learn and practice presentational skills that are relevant to your future as a student and professional. While the concept of the Symposium comes from deep in the past, its format requires you to engage with the modern world of technology. Similarly, while presentations at ancient symposia were limited to a one-room audience, the digital multimedia Symposium Presentation can be an opportunity to reach a wider group of people and practice the skills necessary to take part in conversations at this level.

Symposium Presentations incorporate a good deal of imagery—at least one image on each of the fifteen slides—but we don't expect you to create all these images. This isn't a class on photography or illustration! Instead, this assignment will ask you to find others' images to use in your presentation. As such, an important aspect of the Symposium concerns intellectual property: who owns the rights to photos, videos, or other texts, and under what circumstances those texts can or can't be used in new works. By creating your own text (the Symposium Presentation) in a format that uses materials others have made, you are entering into a realm that requires you to be confident and capable in your understanding of intellectual property. This confidence and capability is part of being a producer in the digital world. Therefore, as part of the Symposium, you will be asked to demonstrate that you understand the intellectual property rights that govern various parts of your presentation.

The Symposium consists of several parts:

Preparing:

Process Posts
From time to time during the semester, you will find and write about images that connect to both your ARP and your Symposium Presentation. These short pieces of writing are called Process Posts. The images you will be asked to find are images that do not merely illustrate topics associated with your research or the course theme, but rather images that raise questions, suggest new ideas, or highlight tensions. The practice of finding these images will lead into image selection for your Symposium Presentation.

The Process Posts will give you an opportunity to reflect on, discuss, and expand the ideas you are thinking about and the variety of images you have found. They will also prove important in allowing you to choose and refine a strong topic for your Symposium Presentation: a topic that is connected to the research for your Analytical Research Project, and that can also be effectively presented within the format and time limits of the project.

The Symposium Presentation:

Selection and Documentation of Appropriate Images
Over the course of the semester, you will work to find and choose the 15 images that will make up the visual part of your Symposium Presentation. You will select images that clearly and powerfully communicate ideas as part of a coherently structured presentation. You will also appropriately cite these images and demonstrate that you understand the rules of copyright that control how they may be used.

Symposium Script
You will provide 50-60 words of text for each of the 15 images you select. This narration, which you will carefully script, will not simply describe or explain your images, but will work with them in order to effectively interest and educate your audience.

Responding:

Symposium Active Listening Response
During the Symposium, you will be required to respond to your classmates' presentations in one of three ways depending on your assignment for a given day. You may be assigned to lead a discussion immediately following the

presentations, to provide immediate written feedback, or to introduce a fellow student's presentation. Your responses will allow you to demonstrate your thoughtfulness as an audience member, and your ability to provide focused, appropriate, and constructive feedback to your classmates.

In the Classroom

A great deal of your work in English 1110 will take the form of consistently active, thoughtful classroom participation. English 1110 is not the kind of class in which it is possible to catch up by memorizing facts out of a textbook, or borrowing notes from another student. You might think of English 1110 as more like playing an instrument or a sport: the ways of thinking, reading, and writing involved are abilities that you need to develop through practice over time. The English 1110 classroom is a place for you to practice these abilities, so that you are prepared to demonstrate them in the "concert" or "game" that your projects represent.

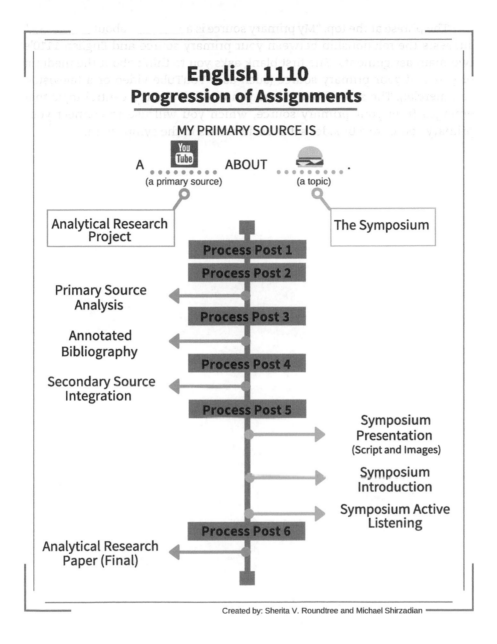

English 1110
Progression of Assignments

MY PRIMARY SOURCE IS

A ⬛YouTube⬛ ABOUT 🍔 .
(a primary source) (a topic)

Analytical Research Project		The Symposium

Process Post 1

Process Post 2

Primary Source Analysis

Process Post 3

Annotated Bibliography

Process Post 4

Secondary Source Integration

Process Post 5

Symposium Presentation
(Script and Images)

Symposium Introduction

Symposium Active Listening

Process Post 6

Analytical Research Paper (Final)

Created by: Sherita V. Roundtree and Michael Shirzadian

Above is an infographic called "English 1110: Progression of Assignments." The infographic depicts the relationships between course assignments—items on the left side belong to the Analytical Research Project and items on the right side belong to the Symposium Presentation. We've included process posts in the middle because they help connect your ARP to your symposium presentation.

The phrase at the top, "My primary source is a _____ about _____,"
suggests the relationship between your primary source and English 1110's
two main assignments. The first blank asks you to think about the medium
or genre of your primary source (such as a YouTube video or a television
commercial). The second blank asks you to think about a central topic that
emerges from your primary source, which you will use to connect your
primary source to a broader set of social issues in the symposium.

CHAPTER 2

Writing Beyond Words

When you read the description of the Symposium in Chapter 1, you may have been surprised to learn that this course—an English course!—will ask you to find and use images in your classwork. This chapter will start by explaining why English 1110 includes multimedia work and then will explain how you can use images in a way that respects the intellectual property of their creators.

'Writing' vs. 'Composition'

At Ohio State, it's very common for students, teachers, and advisors to refer to English 1110 as "First Year Writing." That goes for other colleges and universities, too: 'First Year Writing' is one of many general terms that administrators and professional organizations sometimes use to broadly include the sorts of English courses that college freshmen typically take. And yet, the field of composition studies hasn't considered 'writing' to be limited to mere words on paper for decades. In fact, if you look carefully at your course schedule, you'll see that English 1110 is designated "First Year English Composition." But what does that mean? What's the difference between 'writing' and 'composition'?

When scholars of writing/composition look at the kinds of communication that exist in the modern world, we see a lot of words: books and articles, of course, but also emails, billboards, blog posts, texts, memes, etc. We are awash in a sea of text. This is what we traditionally mean by 'writing': words on a page. As writers ourselves, the authors of this book are very fond of words, and we believe very strongly in their ability to convey rich meaning.

Alongside all these words, however, we see a wide array of images. Books and articles may have photographs and infographics, of course, and these help to illustrate and clarify the points made in the text. But beyond that illustrative function, where images are in a clearly supportive role, in many other types of communication the images are themselves vital parts of the message: a billboard might include an image of the shiny new car the company want you to buy, or a text might include emoji (📝 📕 💯). Sometimes the image is literally the message: for example, someone posts a gif of a slow, sarcastic clap in response to a statement they disagree with.

As teachers of writing, we recognize that 'writing' can't be limited to words. In both our personal and professional lives we make meaning out of words, out of images, and—most powerfully—out of a combination of the two. To recognize the expanded scope of this meaning-making, we tend to talk about 'composition' as a way to include all these non-word means of communication. While the Analytical Research Paper provides practice and training in word-based writing (still the form of communication that is regarded most highly in the university), the English 1110 Symposium will give you practice in composing using images not merely as illustrations, but as vital elements of your message, which will work alongside your words to communicate meanings to your audience.

Intellectual Property: Respecting Others' Creations

So: you're ready to start finding images to use in your Symposium Presentation. Time to open Google Images, right? Well, maybe—but let's take a step back first and talk about copyright.

Whenever someone creates a work of art or intellect—a piece of writing, a song, an image, etc.—it belongs to them, just as much as a physical object they create. We call these works *intellectual property*. As with creators of physical property, intellectual property creators have the right to decide who can use their works, and how. The right of intellectual property creators to control their own work forms the basis of *copyright*: literally, the right to control what happens to any copies (such as digital reproductions or quotations) of their work.

Alongside the word 'copyright', you've probably also seen the phrase "all rights reserved." This is the default for copyright: only the creator of a work has any right to its use, and anyone who wants to use it has to negotiate with the creator (or the owner of the copyright, in some cases) for permission to use the work.

This obviously creates some problems for you in creating a Symposium Presentation, since your instructor is asking you to find images to include in your presentation. However, copyright law does allow for certain kinds of use. Think of papers you've written in the past: you've likely included quotations from other writers' works in order to illustrate or support a point. (We'll cover working with these *secondary sources* in depth in Chapter 5). In the same way that you can often quote from a textual source, you can also use images in your Symposium Presentation and other multimedia work by paying attention to how the creators are distributing them and how you're relating them to your own work.

Fair Use

You might have heard about the idea of a "fair use" of copyrighted materials, especially in an educational setting. But what does that mean? It gets a little complicated, but this is the gist. In general, copyrighted materials for which the creator retains all rights ("all rights reserved") can't be used without the permission of the owner. There are, however, some exceptions to this rule, because our legal system recognizes that there are legitimate reasons why someone might need to use another person's work, even despite 'all rights reserved': that's "fair use."

When dealing with textual materials, there's a long-established legal history of citation under fair use, and for the most part it's fairly uncontroversial: you quote the author in such a way that it's clear to the reader where your writing ends and theirs begins, and you make it clear where your reader can find the whole work if they so desire.

With images, the situation is much more complicated, for two main reasons. First, the photographic and videographic technology available to the average person has evolved far faster than the legal standards governing its use. Only relatively recently has the average person been able to create, transmit, search, and redistribute photographs and other visual content. Remember: the first cameraphone debuted in 2000 and the first multitouch smartphone (the iPhone) not till 2007. YouTube debuted in 2004. These dates don't tell the whole story, of course, but suffice it to say that the kind of widely available image sharing we're now accustomed to is still very new, and our practices as a society just haven't caught up yet.

The other major difference between text and image when it comes to fair use is the scope and character of the work: usually when we quote from a textual document, we use only a tiny, clearly identified snippet, but images are usually used in their entirety, and they may be entirely transformed by adding text, stickers, or other extra elements to them.

Because we use rather different methods in using others' images, compared to those we use with others' words, we have to delve deeper into what qualifies a citation as 'fair use'. The whole thing is quite open to debate—even the legal standards for determining whether a source is used fairly are one big grey area.

The legal standards center on four factors:

- The purpose and character of the use

- The nature of the copyrighted work

- The amount and importance of the portion taken

- The effect of the use on the potential market

Purpose and Character: In considering this factor, courts have discussed how the quoted material functions in the overall work: is it merely copied in, or has it been somehow transformed? Is it just for illustration, or is it being used to make commentary or criticism?

Nature: Usually this boils down to how well-known the quoted material is. Is it from a famous, published work, or is it from an obscure artist who never formally published it?

Amount and Importance: Are you borrowing the entire work, or just a small part of it? And if it's just a portion, are you using the 'heart' of it, the most important or recognizable bit?

Market Effect: Is your use affecting the creator's ability to make money from their creation?

All of these factors play into each other, of course: using an entire image and distributing it for free could impinge on the original's market potential, for example, and using a portion of a pre-existing work has a very different effect on a famous photographer than it does on a hobbyist.

You will probably have noticed that there's no black-and-white way of delineating that a certain use is allowed, while another is forbidden. That's the way the law is written: there is no clear-cut test for whether something is fairly used. A court of law may rule a particular use 'fair' or not, and that might establish a precedent, but in the end it's all rather vague.

If we look at decision records, we see that courts seem to think the most important of these factors is the first: are you somehow transforming the original meaning by adding to it or recontextualizing it? For our purposes, then, it's usually enough to know that you may be able to claim fair use of a copyrighted image, even without its owner's permission, if your purpose is to provide commentary or criticism. For instance, if you are critiquing the way that specific movie posters depict women, or examining how magazine advertisements suggest that products are "cool," you could claim a fair use for the images you're discussing because it's reasonable to show viewers the image in question while providing commentary on it.

If you are interested in using a copyrighted image, you will want to consider carefully whether your use of it would qualify as "fair use." Particularly if you are not commenting on or critiquing the image that you want to use, you may find it helpful to consult two sources from Columbia University:

- *https://copyright.columbia.edu/basics/fair-use.html*
  A more extensive discussion of fair use

- *https://copyright.columbia.edu/basics/fair-use/fair-use-checklist.html*
  The Fair Use Checklist, a form that will help you think through your planned use step-by-step (but will not give you firm yes or no—nothing can)

Alternate Rights Structures: Creative Commons
Not all copyright owners wish to keep "all rights reserved." Instead, they may wish to grant others some rights to encourage sharing. There are a number of

organizations that facilitate that kind of sharing, and Creative Commons (CC) is one of the largest. They have developed a number of copyright licenses that extend rights to others, instead of limiting them.

Why would an intellectual property creator specifically extend rights? Many artists believe that the world of art and expression is made better and richer when creators are able to incorporate others' works into their own, but they also know that copyright restrictions can have what's sometimes called a 'chilling effect': other creators may think they have a valid fair use argument for a particular quotation, but they choose not to go forward with it because they fear litigation. So these artists (photographers, musicians, videographers, writers, etc.) choose not to hold all the rights they're allowed by law, and instead specifically grant them to others under certain conditions.

Let's say you take a great picture and would also like others to use it. By applying a CC license you say, "Go ahead and use it, as long as you acknowledge that I made it." That's the heart of a CC license, but Creative Commons licenses can be customized further to stipulate what others can do with the work. There are four different specifications that can be combined in a license:

BY: Attribution. This is the baseline license, and all CC licenses include this specification, which means that you must acknowledge the initial creator of the image you are using.

ND: No Derivatives. This means that the creator allows you to use the work, but you must use the whole work, unchanged. For a Symposium Presentation, that would mean that, for example, you couldn't use a detail only, or layer the image with another image or with text.

NC: Non-commercial. You can use the image, but not for commercial purposes. Since our Symposium Presentations are educational, this isn't a problem, but you might like to know this if you use CC works in the future.

SA: Share-alike. This means that, if you use the image and choose to distribute your finished product, you must use the same license. Not likely to be an issue with your Symposium Presentations, but good to know.

A word of warning: in most search databases these licenses are applied by the uploader, and no one is checking them. That means that it would be possible to find, for example, a well-known logo uploaded to a sharing site with a CC license designated. In these case, you should use your best judgment: does it seem likely that this user actually had the right to upload this image as their own or is this more likely an error? You don't have to be a detective, tracking IP addresses and digging into the metadata of every image for clues to its origins, but you absolutely do need to use common sense.

Images You Can Just Use: Public Domain Images and Original Works

Certain types of images are always entirely open for you to use, without restriction.

1. Public domain images: An image in the public domain is one for which the original creator no longer retains any rights. Sometimes this happens because the image is so old that copyright has expired, and at other times the creator has explicitly placed the image into the public domain. Certain official documents are also automatically in the public domain, such as works created by the federal government of the United States.

   Works in the public domain are open to use without restriction—the copyright is *public*, meaning that everyone has a right-to-copy. However, you should still cite those images to adhere to academic standards.

2. Original works: Original works are those that *you* have created, whether they are pictures you've taken with a camera, drawn by hand, or made from scratch on a computer. You are the creator of that work, which means you hold all of its copyrights.

   Symposium Presentations are designed to showcase the elements of your research that *you* find intriguing and relevant to the degree that others should hear about them. A successful Symposium Presentation springs from your passion about the topic, and we encourage you to inject this individuality into its composition. One of the best ways to do that is to use images that *you* have created. Using original images in conjunction with original narratives about your research allows for the fullest expression of your thought; a Symposium Presentation full of original work is uniquely yours.

How to Cite Images (in this Class)

While you'll be using MLA citation format for your ARP, we're asking you to use a slightly different format for your Process Post and Symposium Presentation citations:

Author name or username. "Title or filename." License. <URL>

You'll notice that our Symposium Presentation citation format includes the same basic information as any other citation—who created the thing you're citing, what it is, where to find it—but it also includes information on the image's licensing: whether it's Creative Commons, public domain, a fair use of a copyrighted work, or original work. We specifically ask for this information on licensing because it's important to the goals of the Symposium that you not only choose images wisely, but also that you make it clear that you have thought about where it comes from.

A tip: as you move through your educational career, you should remember that different courses and different areas of study use different citation formats. This is the format we're asking you to use for the Symposium Presentation, but it was custom-made for the assignment; for other assignments in other classes, you should always check with your instructor.

How to Cite Fair Use of a Copyrighted Image

Let's say you wished to discuss the internet outrage that occurred when people thought Steven Spielberg had actually killed a triceratops (spoiler: it's a fake dinosaur; the triceratops went extinct 66 million years ago):

Universal Pictures/Everett Collection. "Steven Spielberg with Triceratops."
Copyright: Fair use. <http://www.hollywood.com/general/steven-spielberg-targeted-in-facebook-hunting-prank-59112157/>

For this image it's actually fairly difficult to construct a good citation, but that's why we've chosen it as an example: many of the copyright images you may wish to use will have the same issues.

- *Author name*: This picture has shown up in a number of popular media articles, but never with the original photographer's name listed. However, many of these publications have purchased the right to publish through official channels (a whole separate area of image licensing that you won't get into in your Symposium Presentations), and have listed a copyright notice, so it's fairly easy to find out that Universal Pictures owns the copyright, and licensed the image through the Everett Collection. It would be nice to have the actual photographer's name, but sometimes it's not possible.

- *Image title*: While many images uploaded to sharing sites have an explicit title, images found 'in the wild' often don't. This image doesn't seem to have an official title, so we're just giving it a descriptive title. The purpose of a citation is to help the reader to find the image source, and "Steven Spielberg with Triceratops" will be much more useful to a reader than the filename (another possibility) which in this case is "3822213.JPG"

- *URL*: The image has appeared in many locations, because it was such a viral phenomenon. Usually it's best to figure out what the 'official' location of the image is, but in this case it looks that location is somewhere in the archives of the Everett Collection, which we'd have to pay to access. So instead we're doing the next best thing and using the URL of the article where we found it.

How to Cite Creative Commons Images

Let's say we wanted to use this image, a Lego recreation of a famous scene from *Jurassic Park*, which we found on Flickr:

Here's the citation:

Gabor Lonyai. "Paleontologist at work – LEGO Minifigures, Series 13." CC BY 2.0. <https://www.flickr.com/photos/inetflash/17364482109/>

You'll see that this citation is somewhat simpler than the one for the Spielberg/ Triceratops pic above. If you go to the listed URL, you'll see the photographer's name and the image's title clearly listed on the Flickr page that is the image's official home. Where the Spielberg image needed a Copyright: Fair Use notation (because it was), this image citation needs the short form of its Creative Commons license. (You can refresh your memory on what the different abbreviations mean by looking back a few pages in this chapter.)

How to Cite Original Work

Because you created the image, there is no URL (unless you upload it to Flickr or another site for others to use). Let's say your name is Brutus Buckeye, and you drew a picture of Ohio Stadium. Your citation might read:

Brutus Buckeye. "Ohio Stadium." Original work.

How to Cite Images in the Public Domain

For example, you might wish to use an image of the US Constitution, which is available from the National Archives and Records Administration.

National Archives and Records Administration. "Constitution of the United States, pg. 1." Public Domain. < https://catalog.archives.gov/id/1667751>

Finding Images to Use

We've given you a lot of information about how to cite images, but you might reasonably be wondering, "yes, but where and how do I find these images?" Because databases and their interfaces change so frequently online, we've chosen not to include that information here in this chapter. Instead, your instructor will share a document with you, "How to Find and Identify Images for Your Symposium Presentation."

CHAPTER 3

Rhetoric & Analysis

English 1110 is a class in which you will learn the art of rhetorical analysis. In order to understand what rhetorical analysis involves, you first need to understand what both "rhetoric" and "analysis" mean.

What is Rhetoric?

You may have previously encountered the word "rhetoric" in everyday conversation, as in this example:

> **Trevor**: Look, I've discovered a way to bring dinosaurs back from extinction! I could keep a cute little dinosaur as a pet!
>
> **Lily**: That doesn't sound like a good idea. Do you *want* to end up unleashing velociraptors on the world and having someone make a cautionary movie about you?
>
> **Trevor**: I don't know; that sounds kind of cool.
>
> **Lily**: It was a rhetorical question!

A rhetorical question is a question that does not expect an answer. When Lily asked, "Do you *want* to end up unleashing velociraptors on the world and have someone make a cautionary movie about you?" she was not actually interested in Trevor's answer. Instead, she asked the question to persuade Trevor of her point of view: that bringing dinosaurs back from extinction is not a good idea. In the simplest terms, that is the definition of rhetoric: the use of language to persuade an audience. So a rhetorical question is a question that is used to persuade an audience to agree with a particular view or argument, rather than to seek information.

Another place that we hear the word "rhetoric" in daily life is in politics. We assume that politicians and other public figures should have strong purpose in their speech; that they should be using their words to effect real change. When we suspect that a politician is using the tools of persuasion without any substance to justify their efforts, we may be upset at what appears to be purposeless manipulation. We recognize that such politicians are using "empty rhetoric" or "mere rhetoric," which we often simply shorthand by dismissively calling their speech "rhetoric."

So: understanding rhetoric means understanding how language is used by an author to communicate a message to an audience. This "language" may not always take the form of words—images, sound, and other elements can also be rhetoric! For instance, let's take the example of the politician above. You will probably think differently about a politician who dresses in wingtips, designer sunglasses, and an expensively tailored Italian suit than you would about the same politician if he wore sneakers, blue jeans, and a cowboy hat. Here, clothes are being used to communicate a message to you about what kind of a person the politician is. (At the same time, *context* is an important part of rhetoric: you would probably think that a politician who showed up to a global trade summit in sneakers and blue jeans was being inappropriate, or maybe just rude!)

The Rhetorical Situation: An Author, A Text, and An Audience

A rhetorical situation has three basic parts: an author, a text, and an audience. The author has a relationship with the text, which you might have expected—but the audience has one, too. These can be very different relationships, and can produce very different interpretations of the text. While readers often assume that the author's intended meaning is more important or more "correct" than other interpretations, this is not the case.

Rhetoric can be a part of any medium in which an author is communicating with an audience. Even architecture can be rhetorical! Consider the different impression created by a classical stone building with Grecian columns, and a sleek modern building made of metal and glass. These buildings probably give you different impressions about the type of people who work there, and the type of work that takes place. In other words, the architecture persuades you to think in a certain way by playing on your associations with historical precedents and social functions.

The Greek philosopher Aristotle (384–322 BCE) wrote a guide to rhetoric called, plainly enough, *Rhetoric*—or, from the Latin, *Ars Rhetorica* (*The Art of Rhetoric*). In this book, he broke down the means of persuasion into three major categories: *ethos, logos*, and *pathos*. Today, when we try to understand how a particular text is designed to persuade its audience of a message, we still use these terms and categories, saying that a text is appealing to logic (*logos*), or to emotion (*pathos*), or to the speaker's trustworthiness or character (*ethos*).

Ethos

Ethos is a means of persuasion that has to do with the person making the argument. When *ethos* is used as a means of persuasion, the audience is persuaded to accept the argument because they trust the person who is making it. For instance, you would probably trust a toothpaste recommendation that comes from a dentist, or a vitamin recommendation from a doctor! You might also trust an athlete who promotes a sneaker or a sports drink, or a musician who endorses a particular guitar. Sometimes trust comes from knowledge of a person's experience. Sometimes it comes from prestige: for instance, you might trust the Surgeon General of the United States more than another doctor; you might also trust an article published by the *New York Times* more than one published by a tabloid such as *Us Weekly*. An important part of *ethos* can also be production values: the impression of quality, accuracy, and appropriateness given by the "language" of a text itself. If you are familiar with the low-budget law office advertisements that often run on late-night television in America, you probably understand how production values can affect your willingness to trust an author!

It is important to understand that *ethos* is artificial. Though we often use the word "artificial" as a criticism, in fact it simply means *made by skill*. In other words, *ethos* is something that the author constructs through the choices that he or she makes in creating the text. This does not mean that the *ethos* is always what the author intends! The author's construction of *ethos* may be more or less successful. This is why it is important for you, as an author, to be aware of how your choices work to enhance or detract from your *ethos*.

Logos

Logos is a means of persuasion that has to do with the logical presentation of undeniable facts. For example, scientific arguments that rely on laboratory evidence or unbiased observation persuade their audience through *logos*. If your friend argues that you should not drive in a heavy snowstorm, he or she might employ *logos* by informing you that it is difficult to drive in snow, and that a large number of car accidents occur in snowstorms; thus, if you drive in the snowstorm, you are likely to suffer an accident.

Again, it is important to remember that *logos* is a persuasive technique that is used by a speaker or author, and not a "natural" or "automatic" property of a particular text or fact. While evidence may exist outside of an argument, individual authors and speakers choose specific facts to employ for their persuasive purposes.

Pathos

Pathos is a means of persuasion that has to do with emotion. (*Pathos* and the more common word "pathetic" originally come from the same Greek and Latin words as "passion," and all have to do with suffering and other strong emotions.) Authors who use *pathos* may intend for their audience to feel fear, joy, sadness, homesickness, or loneliness, as a few examples. An animal shelter may run an advertisement that features images of abandoned kittens or puppies that need new homes; an insurance company may show a family losing their home to a terrible storm; a computer advertisement might suggest that parents and children separated by long distances can be reunited through their use of technology. In each of these cases, the author of the advertisement wants to make the viewer feel things: sad for the adorable animals that need to be rescued; fearful that their own family might be threatened; longing for their own parents or children.

Most people do not realize how common *pathos* is as a persuasive technique. Much of advertising relies on bypassing your logical and intellectual faculties in favor of your emotions, so as to cause you to desire something. Desire is a very powerful emotion! However, *pathos* is also frequently used in politics. Politicians use *pathos* to appeal to citizens' love and pride in their country, but also to appeal to their fear of war, terrorism, or poverty. *Pathos* can be a way to encourage audiences to make decisions based on feelings rather than facts, which is often very valuable in the political arena.

Ethos, Logos, and Pathos in the ARP

The Analytical Research Project asks you to carefully examine the rhetoric of your primary source. You will be responsible for understanding how the author of your primary source persuades the audience to accept a certain meaning. This may include investigating how persuasive techniques are employed. For instance: if an advertisement seems to be designed to produce an emotional response from its audience, how has the advertisement been designed to produce that response? What aspects of the advertisement create that effect? Why do they create that effect? And towards what audience are they targeted? Similarly, if you are examining a primary source that relies on *ethos*: why was this particular technique chosen? How does the primary source communicate and highlight the *ethos* of the spokesperson or author?

However, it is also important to remember that the Analytical Research Project makes you into an author. You too are creating a text through your work. As an author, you will be responsible for persuading your audience to accept your argument. Therefore, you must employ persuasive techniques.

From the first word of your Analytical Research Paper, you will be building your own *ethos*. Through your word choices, your command of the conventions of academic writing, your ability to effectively employ evidence, and the accuracy and sophistication of your observations, you will strive to convince the reader that you must be taken seriously as a writer and as a thinker. The "production values" of your paper—the skill with which you employ appropriate punctuation, grammar, attribution, and diction—will be used by the reader to determine your trustworthiness.

You will also rely on *logos* to persuade your reader. You will present neutral observations about your primary source as evidence for your claims, just as a scientist in the laboratory makes unbiased observations. It will be vital for you to present these observations in a clear and logical order, so that a reader will be inclined to accept your argument. You will also use evidence from secondary sources as a way to strengthen your claims.

Pathos is the persuasive technique least likely to appear in your Analytical Research Paper; in fact, to employ *pathos* in a piece of analytical writing (where it is seldom appropriate) would most likely weaken your *ethos* as an academic writer. However, you may find *pathos* to be a valuable tool as you approach your Symposium Presentation.

What is Analysis?

Rhetoric is what you will learn to investigate in English 1110. The means through which you will investigate it is analysis.

The word "analysis" comes from the Greek word *analusis*, which has to do with solving or unraveling. When you perform analysis, you are doing just this: unraveling a knot, solving a mystery, making something murky clear. To analyze something is to investigate *how* and *why* it is the way it is—to seek to understand the way it is working.

Analysis is a process that involves observing, asking questions, and synthesizing meaningful answers. You might think of this process as similar to detective work. A detective visits the scene of a crime and carefully inspects it. He or she will have questions about certain parts of the crime scene: why was this window left open? If it was a rainy night, why is there no trace of rain on the carpet? Why did the burglar alarm not go off? A very famous Arthur Conan Doyle story, "Silver Blaze," sees Sherlock Holmes solve a mystery by observing a very important detail and asking the right question about it: a guard dog did not bark while a robbery was taking place. Why did the dog not bark? (The answer: because the robber was someone the dog knew!)

It is important to remember that the criminal, in this example, has not deliberately encoded a secret message about his or her identity. What the detective is looking for is any information that might help him or her understand what took place at the scene. Some of this information might, in fact, have nothing to do with the criminal or the crime, but might instead raise important questions about the history, people, and places involved. The detective is primarily looking for information that seems like it will improve his or her understanding. The analyst does the same.

Of course, you—as an analyst—have a great advantage over a detective: there is no one "true" or "accurate" meaning that you are trying to discover. There is no criminal whom you have to lock up. Instead, your goal is simply to offer a convincing explanation of how and why a particular situation has been created.

Sometimes, the meaning of the details you observe may not be immediately obvious. While some meanings are **explicit**, others are **implicit**.

Explicit meanings or messages are directly shown or expressed. You have probably heard the word *explicit* used to describe violent or sexual content in movies or video games. When people talk about explicit violence or sexual content, they mean that this content is actually shown onscreen. An explicit message is, similarly, a message that is expressed rather than suggested.

Implicit meanings or messages are meanings or messages that are suggested, but not actually shown. For instance, in the past, movies were not allowed to show certain kinds of violence or sexual content. Instead, they might *suggest* that such events had taken place—for instance, by showing two people kissing passionately, then cutting to a scene of them having breakfast together the next morning. This would *imply* that something racier had happened, without actually saying so. Implicit messages expect the audience to understand what they are suggesting, and can be a very powerful (and purposeful) means of persuasion.

It's also possible for a text to imply a meaning or message that the author did not directly intend. An author's choice of words might inadvertently imply that the author holds a certain belief or worldview, even if the author's intent was not to communicate this—and even if the author is not aware of this implication. In such cases, it's important to remember that implicit messages and meanings are not secret or deliberately hidden. They are not the result of the author encoding meanings. Remember: an author's intentions may or may not be in line with an audience's interpretation of a text! It might be helpful to imagine a man taking a walk across a wet field: his purpose is to take a walk, not to leave a track of his movements. Nevertheless, we can try to understand his route and his destination by reading his footprints.

Learning to perform strong, careful analysis means training your mind to constantly observe details, ask questions, and consider implicit and explicit meanings. It means understanding how to make connections between the observations and answers that you find. One term for this is *synthesis*, which literally means "putting things together." When you synthesize an idea, you put many small observations together to form a larger, more complex theory.

For instance: the detective who hopes to solve a mystery is not content to simply find answers to his or her questions about what he or she observes. It is not enough for Sherlock Holmes to know that the robber in "Silver Blaze" was someone that the guard dog knew. He must combine this answer with other observations and ideas in order to synthesize a theory about who the robber is!

Rhetorical Analysis

Now that you understand the nature of rhetoric and the principles of analysis, you may find yourself asking how you are supposed to put the two together, as the Analytical Research Project demands. That is: what does it mean to use analysis to solve the "mysteries" of rhetoric?

Remember: analysis investigates *how* and *why* something is the way it is. In the case of rhetoric, analysis seeks to uncover *how* and *why* a particular meaning is communicated. What choices has the author of a text made, and why do you think the author has made those choices? How do you think the audience will interpret those choices? Why do you think the audience will interpret those choices in that way?

Before you engage in rhetorical analysis, you should be aware of two common mistakes:

It Just Is The "It just is" mistake assumes that some details in texts don't mean anything—that they are unplanned, accidental or coincidental, and therefore don't need to be questioned or understood. If you remember our discussion of analysis as a kind of detective work, then you may remember how every detail at a crime scene may reveal something about the world of the crime. The job of the detective is to try, as best as possible, to come up with a theory that explains how this world got to be the way that it is. Every detail tells you something about this world.

They Didn't Mean It That Way It is common for people to argue that certain details either don't need to be questioned or must be understood in a certain way. This is because "they didn't mean it that way." In other words, the authors of the text did not intend for the text to be analyzed or understood in this way. A good way to come to see the flaw in this reasoning might be to think of a case when someone (a corporate advertisement, a parent, a teacher) has said something that they think is "cool" or "hip," but that is actually hilariously embarrassing. The fact that this person's intention was to seem cool does not alter the fact that what they said was hilariously embarrassing! In fact, were you analyzing their use of rhetoric, you would probably want to explore both the possible intention of the author (to seem cool) and the likely effect on the audience (embarrassing). Remember that an author and a reader can have very different relationships to the text.

It is sometimes useful to identify various rhetorical parts of a text, in order to understand how the text is working. While rhetoricians since the days of Aristotle have offered many different names for the elements of rhetoric, here are a few terms that you may find helpful:

The claim: The claim is the main argument that the author is making. It is the point that the author wants to persuade the audience to accept. In an academic paper, this is usually called the thesis.

The context: The context is the environment in which the text is created or encountered—the events and atmosphere *around* the text. The context may be a particular time, a particular place, a particular moment in political or cultural life, or anything else that affects how the text is made or received.

The current: Sometimes, a text specifically positions itself as responding to a popular belief or argument. This belief or argument is the current that the text is going against. An example of a current might be found in an advertisement that declares, "They said it couldn't be done!" In this case, "their" insistence that "it couldn't be done" is set up as a current that the advertisement can then push against—presumably by then showing you that its product has done the impossible (creating even bigger hamburgers, even spicier chips, or something of the sort).

Some Examples

Take a moment to read the following examples, considering how you might identify the claim, the context, and—if either of these articles makes use of it—the current.

Invasion of the Hedge Fund Almonds
Tom Philpott for Mother Jones

[...] Almond products—snack mixes, butters, milk—are flying off supermarket shelves. The value of the California almond market hit $4.8 billion in 2012—that's triple the level of a decade earlier. Only dairy is worth more to the state than almonds and grapes. In fact, almonds, along with California-grown pistachios and walnuts, are becoming so lucrative that big investment funds, eager to get in on the boom, are snapping up land and dropping in trees.

There's just one problem: Almond orchards require about a third more water per acre than grape vineyards. In fact, they're one of California's thirstiest crops. It takes a gallon of water to produce a single almond—more than three times the amount required for a grape and two and a half times as much for a strawberry. There's more water embedded in just four almonds than there is in a full head of lettuce. But unlike row crops, which farmers can choose not to plant during dry spells, almond trees must be watered no matter what.

In the midst of the worst drought in California's history, you might expect almonds' extreme thirst to be a deal breaker. But it's not. In fact, the drought has had hardly any impact at all on the almond boom. The state's farmers bought at least 8.33 million young almond trees between July 2013 and July 2014, a 25 percent increase from the previous year. About a quarter of the saplings went to replace old orchards, but most of the rest were new plantings, some 48,000 acres' worth, an area equal to three Manhattans.

In order to thrive, almond trees need a Mediterranean climate, hot summers and mild winters. Those come free in the Central Valley. But steady access to water is just as crucial to an almond grove's success. So where is the water for all these new orchards coming from? No longer California's famed irrigation projects, which draw on the state's rivers and have slowed to a trickle during the drought. Instead, farmers are tapping into groundwater.

In all of the other water-scarce states in the West, authorities restrict how much water a user can pump out of the ground. But in California, landowners can drop a well wherever they want, unimpeded by the state... As the State Water Resources Control Board puts it on its website, "To get a right to groundwater, you simply extract the water and use it for a beneficial purpose."

As a result, Central Valley farmers have for years been drawing down groundwater at an alarming rate. Between 2003 and 2010, the valley's aquifers lost a total of 20 cubic kilometers of groundwater—enough to meet the household water needs of New York City for 11 years.

And then came the current drought, which started in 2011, when suddenly the region's groundwater was being pumped up at an estimated rate of nearly seven cubic kilometers per year... Meanwhile, several recent studies suggest that the West is actually in the early stages of a multidecade "megadrought."

Experts worry that the combination of overpumping and drought could be catastrophic for the Central Valley, whose economy depends on being one of the world's most productive farming areas. Richard Howitt, an agricultural economist at the University of California-Davis Center for Watershed Sciences, told me that he considers the situation "a slow-moving train wreck."

Beyond Almonds: A Rogue's Gallery of Guzzlers in California's Drought
Dan Charles for *NPR*

California is parched. Wells are running dry. Vegetable fields have been left fallow and lawns are dying. There must be some villain behind all this, right?

Both Slate and Mother Jones have reported that almonds are sucking California dry. Each innocent-looking nut, we learn, robs the land of an entire gallon of water. All told, California's almonds consume three times more water than the entire city of Los Angeles. And their thirst is growing, year by year. California's farmers continue to convert new swaths of land to almond orchards.

Case closed? Maybe not, Grist retorts. Almonds get a lot of attention because production of them has been booming. And it's true that they do consume more water, per acre, than many other crops (though not all). Vineyards use much less water than almonds, and most vegetables also require less irrigation.

But that's only if you calculate water use in gallons per acre or gallons per pound of product. There's a different, and probably better, way to calculate water efficiency. How about water consumption *per unit of value created?* Gallons used per dollar of production, say. By that measure, almonds look just great, because they are so valuable.

So there's a very good argument that almonds are exactly what California's farmers *should* be growing with their precious water.

There is one problem with almonds, though. They're trees. They last for years, and they need water every single year, whether it's wet or dry. Farmers who've devoted their land to production of almonds (or walnuts and pistachios) can't easily adapt to water shortages. Letting the trees die would be a catastrophe, so they sometimes pay exorbitant prices or dig ever-deeper wells.

Water experts like Jay Lund, from the University of California, Davis, say that in the future, California should take care to maintain a healthy mix of trees and annual crops like vegetables. In drought years, farmers could then decide not to plant their tomato fields, freeing up water for their trees.

In the first article, the author explicitly identifies several key elements of context, including (1) a cultural moment at which almond products are extremely popular, leading investment firms to invest in them, and (2) a massive drought in California. The claim of his article seems to be that it would be rational for California farmers to cut back on almond production, which uses a lot of water, and that the failure of farmers to do so has troubling environmental implications. (The author cites experts who worry "that the combination of overpumping and drought could be catastrophic for the Central Valley," and that the situation is "a slow-moving train wreck.")

In the second article, the author explicitly identifies several of the same key elements of context. "California is parched. Wells are running dry... California's farmers contine to convert new swaths of land to almond orchards." However, the claim that this article is making is different! "[T]here's a very good argument," this author writes, "that almonds are exactly what California's farmers *should* be growing with their precious water." In fact, this article seems to be written to go against the *current* of which the first article is a part: the popular belief that there is a "villain" behind the California drought, and that the villain is the thirsty almond.

Consider how each of these articles presents its argument. Given that each article is making a different argument, why do they use so many of the same details? Where do they differ? What does their rhetoric tell you?

Rhetorical Analysis in the ARP

The Analytical Research Project asks you to perform one single, very thorough piece of rhetorical analysis: the rhetorical analysis of your primary source. Step-by-step, throughout the project, you will engage with the process of moving from analytical summary of your primary source to a well-researched investigation and, ultimately, an analytical argument about your primary source's rhetoric.

In order to accomplish this task, you will learn several **heuristics** that will help you practice and hone your analytical abilities. "Heuristic" comes from the Greek word *heuriskein* that means "to find or discover." Heuristics are methods that help you find or discover solutions to problems. In the next chapter, we will investigate heuristics that will help you to find, question, and interpret important details in your primary source.

CHAPTER 4

The Art of Analysis

When you set out to analyze a text, where do you begin? For many people, this may seem like a question that has an obvious answer. You look at a text and "know" what the text is about through that first look. It may seem as though all of the meaning of a text is immediately visible on the surface—and as though you, the audience, are passively receiving the meaning of the text. (Something that is *passive* has an action done to it, in contrast to something *active*, which acts.) If this were the case, then perhaps the question of how to start analyzing a text would indeed be very obvious—you would simply look at the text very hard until you saw everything that there was to see about it.

However, what you may not realize is that you are not a passive audience. Even though you may *feel* that you are passively consuming a text, the meaning of a text is something that you actively help to produce every time you read a book, view a video, or look at an image. This means that the process of analysis involves not only looking very closely at a text, but also looking very closely at *you*.

When you begin analyzing a text, you will want to understand how your own assumptions, expectations, and opinions may be affecting your experience of that text. You might think of these factors as having the power to change how much or how little you see of the text. It's important to note that no one sees the "whole" text—in other words, no one sees any text without *some* assumptions, expectations, and opinions. However, when you are performing analysis, it will be important for you to be aware of how your observations are affected by these factors.

Here, we have outlined several key ways in which you may find yourself limited in your view of a text. We have called these *Walls*. In building design, walls are barriers that limit what you can see in a space and how you can move through it. Your analytical walls are ways of thinking that prevent you from seeing parts of a text. Just as an occupant of a building may be unaware of what is happening beyond the building's walls, you may be unaware—until you recognize your analytic walls—that you are missing part of the text.

We have also offered several key ways to combat walls. We have called these *Windows*. Windows allow you to see the world outside of your own walls—whether those walls are the walls of a house, a car, an airplane, or simply the walls of your own experience. These windows are meant to help you find new ways to see parts of a text that you may previously have ignored or missed.

Finally, we have offered a step-by-step strategy for approaching practical analysis, taken from the textbook *Writing Analytically*. This strategy features **Five Analytical Moves** that will lead you through starting to effectively see a text.

Walls

Assumptions

An assumption is an idea that you accept without question. It may be so natural to you that you have never paused to consider why you believe that it is true. Often, assumptions are strongly rooted in what we hear and see around us. For instance, a child who has grown up in a suburban house in an American city may assume that it is normal or natural for families to live in houses with lawns on suburban streets. That child might be very surprised by the idea that most families live in very different settings. A student who comes from a community where it is common for high school graduates to attend college thousands of miles from home may assume that it is normal or natural for teenagers to do this—despite the fact that for many people, this idea would be startling!

When it comes to texts, many of our assumptions have to do with what we consider normal or natural to see represented in media. It is easy to see the world that is depicted in movies and on TV as "natural"—that is, it is simply the way the world is. Of course, we would never assume that we live in a world full of giant robots and superheroes, but very often we think that these are the only significant differences between the "real" world and the screen world. This can lead us to accept many ideas that analysis requires us to question. For instance: famously, most television shows set in New York City depict characters who have low-pressure jobs, lots of spending money, and enormous apartments. If we assume that this is simply "natural," and that this is the way all people in New York City live, then we fail to see that these details are significant—and therefore fail to ask important questions about them.

Of course, authors of texts also have assumptions that limit their own views. Identifying the assumptions that authors have made can be extremely helpful, particularly when it comes to dealing with secondary sources. When you understand an author's assumptions, you can effectively challenge them—a strong way of introducing your own ideas into a critical conversation.

Starting with the End

When you are engaged in the work of analysis, it can be very tempting to assume that you know from the start what your conclusion will be. Many of us place great stock in our first impressions, and are reluctant to admit that we do not know "the right answer." However, when you pre-select an answer—that is, when you assume you know what a text means before you have done any analytical work—you prevent yourself from seeing other possible answers. You may see only what fits easily into your preconceived notions, neglecting significant details that do not fit with your interpretation or "answer."

When effectively done, analysis should be a process of discovery. By its very nature, discovery means not knowing precisely what it is that you will find. You may have an idea of which direction you want to go in—but not precisely what you will find along the route, or where you will end up at the end of it.

One powerful reason that people jump to conclusions or pre-select a text's meaning can be their belief that this interpretation is somehow "correct": that it is what their teacher, or another authority figure, wants to see. It is important to understand that your teacher, in English 1110, does not have a list of correct interpretations hidden in his or her desk. A successful interpretation is the one that you arrive at after careful analytical work, not the one that seems most likely to please.

Opinions and Evaluations

When you and your best friend have just finished watching a movie, your best friend may turn to you and ask, "So, what did you think?" It seems unlikely that you would have much trouble answering this question, and your answer would probably begin with an opinion: "I liked it!" or "I hated it!" or "I thought it was good," or "I thought it was terrible."

Therefore, when your teacher asks you what you think about a text, you might think—particularly if that text is part of a TV show or movie!—that he or she is asking you to offer the same sort of answer.

However, personal opinions rarely make useful analytical observations. This is because they are not observations about the text—they are observations about you and your response to the text. They take your attention away from what is actually happening in the text, and instead focus your attention on your own experience. Since your goal is to better understand what is happening in the text, you can see how this would be an obstacle.

Similarly, you might assume that your teacher is asking you to offer a judgment about the text—that is, that he or she wants you to evaluate how well or badly the text is accomplishing its function. This assumption is particularly natural if you frequently read movie, music, or TV reviews, in which the goal of the author is to assess the quality of the text.

You, however, have a different goal: to make an analytical argument about the text. Since this is the case, making judgments about the text is counterproductive—it may prevent you from seeing other possibilities.

It's a good idea to keep a close eye out for any "opinion words" that might indicate you are straying into this realm of personal judgment. Words like "good," "bad," "fantastic," "terrible," "wonderful" and "awful" should probably not be used to describe your text—even if you may privately agree with them.

Windows

Asking Questions

The single most important habit that you can develop when engaged in analytical research is the habit of asking questions. In many ways, you could describe this as a strategy of looking for the unknown. What *don't* you know about the text you are analyzing?

This can be a particularly effective strategy for combating assumptions because an assumption often conceals a question you did not know you had. For example, building on some of the examples of assumptions that we previously discussed: let's say that you watch a TV advertisement that features a young family that lives in a large suburban house. If you assume that it is simply normal for all families to live in large suburban houses, you are unable to see an important question: why have the authors of this advertisement chosen to show a family in this particular setting, as opposed to an urban or a rural environment?

Once you begin training yourself to ask questions, you will find them almost everywhere. As an exercise, try looking at the advertisement on the next page and finding five questions to ask about it.

What questions did you come up with about this advertisement? Make sure that the questions you are asking are questions about what you see in the advertisement! Some examples of questions you might ask about this advertisement are:

- Who is the man in the advertisement? How do I know? Why does this man feature in the advertisement?

- What does the word "revolutionary" suggest in this advertisement?

- Why is there so much emphasis on kites in this advertisement?

- Why has Apple chosen to ask what kind of *man* owns his own computer, rather than what kind of *person*?

- Why does the advertisement show a computer in an eighteenth century room, which would seem to be a strange and impossible scene?

Start at the Beginning

If you have ever worked a jigsaw puzzle, you probably know that the most effective way to begin is not by looking at the picture on the box and trying to see it in the disassembled pieces, but rather by looking at the pieces themselves and seeing how they relate to and differ from each other. Some pieces are flat-edged to form a border; some may share a particular color, or seem to have the same line running through them. At some point, it will be useful to think about how these groups of pieces combine to form the big picture. However, at the beginning, the best strategy is to forget the big picture.

Similarly, when it comes to analysis, the best strategy is to avoid trying to fit the pieces into a certain "big picture." Instead, become comfortable starting at the beginning: by sorting through the pieces of your text and noticing clear patterns that connect them to one another. The 5 Analytical Tools that you will learn in this chapter will help you acquire a method for doing this. However, it is up to you to cultivate a habit of mind that will allow you to curiously and open-mindedly explore the details of your text without attempting to look ahead and limit what those details can mean.

It's Not Personal

When you are performing analysis, your goal is to analyze a text—not to analyze your own experience of a text. It's important to remember that not everyone will share your experience! Other people may understand things that you find confusing, disagree with your assumptions, make different assumptions, and be confused by things that you understand! You should make sure not to *privilege* your own experience. When we use the word "privilege" in this sense, it means giving special importance or priority. You should not assume that your own experience is the natural or correct experience of a text, simply because it is yours.

This does not mean that you can never take your own responses into consideration. Your own responses may, in fact, be very valuable! However, you should ask yourself: What in this text makes me respond to it like this? Would other people respond to this text in the same way? How might other people respond, and what in this text might cause them to respond that way? You may find that your own 1110 classroom is the most valuable place for you to investigate these questions. You share this classroom with students from a variety of different backgrounds. It is very likely that they respond to a text in very different ways. What can you learn about a text by considering their responses? What can you learn about your own response?

In other words, you do not have to remove yourself from analysis— and, in fact, if you think back on what we've talked about in this chapter, you'll probably come to the conclusion that it would be impossible to do so! However, you should try to see a text from many perspectives—not only your own.

One strategy for examining or breaking down your own responses to a text is asking: Why? For example, let's return to the sample Apple advertisement on page [34]. How might you go about breaking down your response to this advertisement?

> **You**: I think this advertisement is really funny.
> **Your inner analyst**: Why?
> **You**: It shows Benjamin Franklin looking at a computer! That's ridiculous!
> **Your inner analyst**: Why?
> **You**: Well, Benjamin Franklin lived in the eighteenth century, when there were no computers. But he's looking at a twentieth-century computer. That's impossible, and the idea of an eighteenth-century guy playing with a twentieth-century computer is funny.
> **Your inner analyst**: Why?
> **You**: It's really advanced technology, and he's an eighteenth-century guy! Would he even know how to use it? It would blow his mind!

At this point, you have made several observations about the advertisement that could lead in fruitful analytical directions. (Why has the advertisement chosen to show an "eighteenth-century guy" using really advanced technology, despite the fact that such a scene is impossible? What does the contrast between the eighteenth-century scene and the computer suggest?) By refusing to simply describe the advertisement as "funny," and instead focusing on what details in the advertisement combine to produce this response for you, you have started to engage in analysis!

You'll get further in analysis, however, if you go in with a game plan. Below, we've included a section from *Writing Analytically* that details a set of strategies for analyzing most sorts of text, from word-based texts to images and videos.

The Five Analytical Moves

The act of analyzing can be broken down into five essential moves:

> Move 1: Suspend judgment.
> Move 2: Define significant parts and how they are related.
> Move 3: Make the implicit explicit. Push observations to implications by ASKING "SO WHAT?"
> Move 4: Look for patterns of repetition and contrast and for anomalies (THE METHOD).
> Move 5: Keep reformulating questions and explanations.

Move 1: Suspend Judgment

A lot of what passes for thinking is merely reacting: right/wrong, good/bad, loved it/hated it, couldn't relate to it, boring. Responses like these are habits, reflexes of the mind. And they are surprisingly tough habits to break. Experiment: eavesdrop on people walking out of a movie. Most of them will immediately voice their approval or disapproval, usually in either/or terms: "I think it was a good movie and you are wrong to think it was bad." And so on.

A first move in conducting analysis—in fact, a precondition—is to delay judgment, especially of the agree-disagree, like-dislike kind. In the opening pages of *The Great Gatsby*, Nick Carraway cites as the one piece of wisdom he learned from his father the following statement: "Reserving judgments is a matter of infinite hope." In analysis the goal is always to understand before you judge.

Move 2: Define Significant Parts and How They Are Related

In order to define significant parts and figure out how they are related, writers need to train themselves to attend closely to details. Becoming observant is not natural; it's learned. Toward that end, this book offers a series of observation and interpretation strategies to equip you to see more and to make more of what you see.

The first of these is a strategy we call NOTICE & FOCUS, which will help you to stay open longer to what you can notice in your subject matter. Do this by starting not with "What do I think?" or, worse, with "What do I like/dislike?" but with "What do I *notice?*" This small shift in words will engineer the major conceptual shift this chapter asks you to make: to locate more of your time and attention in the observation stage, which necessarily precedes formulating a thesis.

Notice & Focus: SLOW DOWN

Not "What do you think?" &

Not "What do you like or dislike?"

but

"What do you notice?"

A few prompts:

What do you find most INTERESTING?

What do you find most STRANGE?

What do you find most REVEALING?

© Cengage Learning®

This exercise is governed by repeated return to the question, "What do you notice?". Most people's tendency is to generalize and thus rapidly move away from whatever it is they are looking at. The question "What do you notice?" redirects attention to the subject matter, itself, and delays the pressure to come up with answers (see Figure 4.1).

1	**Repeatedly answer the question, "What do you notice?,"** being sure to cite actual details of the thing being observed rather than moving to more general observations about it. (This is more difficult than it sounds.) This phase of the exercise should produce an extended and unordered list of details—features of the thing being observed—that call attention to themselves for one reason or another.
2	**Rank (create an order of importance) for the various features you have noticed.** Answer the question "What three details (specific features of the subject matter) are most interesting (or significant or revealing or strange)?" The purpose of relying on "interesting" or one of the other suggested words is that these will help to deactivate the like/dislike switch, which is so much a reflex in all of us, and replace it with a more analytical perspective.
3	**Say why the three things you selected struck you as the most interesting.** Remember to start by noticing as much as you can about what you are looking at. Dwell with the data. Record what you see. Don't move to generalization or judgment. What this procedure will begin to demonstrate is how useful description is as a tool for arriving at ideas. Stay at the description stage longer (in that attitude of uncertainty we've recommended) and have better ideas. Training yourself to notice is fun. It will improve your memory as well as your ability to think.

© 2015 Cengage Learning®

FIGURE 4.1
Notice & Focus + Ranking

Remember to start by noticing as much as you can about what you are looking at. Dwell with the data. Record what you see. It will improve your memory as well as your ability to think.

"Interesting," "Revealing," "Strange"

These three words are triggers for analysis. Often we are interested by things that have captured our attention without our clearly knowing why. To say that something is interesting is not the end but the beginning of analysis. If you press yourself to explain why something is interesting, revealing, or strange, you will be prompted to make an analytical move.

Revealing (or *significant*) requires you to make choices that can lead to interpretive leaps. If something strikes you as revealing or significant, even if you're not yet sure why, you will eventually begin producing some explanation. The word *strange* gives us permission to notice oddities and things that initially seem not to fit. *Strange*, in this context, is not a judgmental term, but one denoting features of a subject that aren't readily explainable. Where you locate something strange, you have isolated something to figure out—what makes it strange and why.

Noticing and Rhetorical Analysis

When you become attuned to noticing words and details rather than registering general impressions, you inevitably focus not only on the message—what gets said—but on how things get said. To notice how information is delivered is to focus on its rhetoric. To analyze the rhetoric of something is to assess how that something persuades or positions us as readers or viewers or listeners.

Rhetorical analysis is an essential skill because it reveals how voices in the world are perennially seeking to enlist our support and shape our behavior.

Everything has a rhetoric, not just political speeches and not even just words: classrooms, churches, supermarkets, department store windows, Starbucks, photographs, magazine covers, your bedroom, this book. Intention, by the way, is not the issue. It doesn't matter whether the effect of a place or a piece of writing on its viewers (or readers) is deliberate and planned or not. What matters is that you can notice how the details of the thing itself encourage or discourage certain kinds of responses in the "consumers" of whatever it is you are studying.

What, for example, does the high ceiling of a Gothic cathedral invite in the way of response from people who enter it? How might the high ceilings make people feel about their places in the world? What do the raised platform at the front of a classroom and the tidy rows of desks secured to the floor say to the students who enter there?

To get you started on rhetorical analysis, here is a brief example on the layout of our college campus.

> The campus is laid out in several rows and quadrangles. It is interesting to observe where the different academic buildings are, relative to the academic departments they house. It is also interesting to see how the campus positions student housing. In a way, the campus is set up as a series of quadrangles—areas of space with four sides. One of the dormitories, for example, forms a quadrangle. Quadrangles invite people to look in—rather than out. They are enclosed spaces, the center of which is a kind of blank. The center serves as a shared space, a safely walled-off area for the development of a separate community. The academic buildings also form a quadrangle of sorts, with an open green space in the center. On one side of the quadrangle are the buildings that house the natural and social sciences. Opposite these—on the other side of a street that runs through the center of campus—are the modern brick and glass structures that house the arts and the humanities....

What might these details lead us to conclude about the rhetoric of the campus layout?

- that the campus is inward-looking and self-enclosed
- that it invites its members to feel separate and safe
- that it announces the division of the sciences and the social sciences from the arts and humanities, so the campus layout arguably creates the sense of a divided community.

Doing Exploratory Writing in the Observation Stage: Freewriting

What is especially useful about so-called "prewriting" strategies such as NOTICE & FOCUS is freedom—freedom to experiment without worrying about readers saying that you are wrong, freedom to just pay attention to what you notice and to see where these observations might lead you. But NOTICE & FOCUS and other forms of listing can also arrest you in the list stage: you have your column of ranked observations, but now what?

The answer to that last question is to start writing consecutive sentences explaining why you found particular details especially interesting and revealing. Your goal at this stage is not to produce a finished paper, but to start some trains of thought on features of your subject that seem worth writing about.

The name that is most often attached to this kind of exploratory writing— which can, by the way, happen at various points in the writing process, not just at the beginning—is "freewriting."

"How Do I Know What I Think Until I See What I Say?" Freewriting is a method of arriving at ideas by writing continuously about a subject for a limited period of time without pausing to edit or revise. The rationale behind this activity can be understood through a well-known remark by the novelist E.M. Forster (in regard to the "tyranny" of prearranging everything): "How do I know what I think until I see what I say?" Freewriting gives you the chance to see what you'll say.

The writer Anne Lamott writes eloquently (in *Bird by Bird*) about the censors we all hear as nasty voices in our heads that keep us from writing. These are the internalized voices of past critics whose comments have become magnified to suggest that we will never get it right. Freewriting allows us to tune out these voices long enough to discover what we might think.

Freewriting opens up space for thinking by enabling us to catch different thoughts as they occur to us, without worrying prematurely about how to communicate these to a reader. The order in which ideas occur to us is not linear. Things rarely line up in a straight, forward-moving sequence. As we try to pursue one thought, others press on our attention. The act of writing allows us to follow our mental trails and to experiment with alternate routes without losing track of where we've been. Without writing, in all but the most carefully trained memories, the trails keep vanishing, sometimes leaving us stranded.

In paper-writing, you are required to develop ideas sequentially. In freewriting you have the freedom to make sudden, often unanticipated leaps. These frequently take you from a bland, predictable statement to an insight. You learn what you think by seeing what you say.

Freewriting seeks to remove what the rhetorician Peter Elbow saw as the primary cause of much poor writing: the writer's attempt to conduct two essentially opposed activities—drafting and editing, inventing and arranging—at the same time. Freewriting helps you to separate these activities until you've generated enough material to actually be worth arranging for an audience.

In general, only the most practiced analytical thinkers can arrive at their best ideas before they begin to write. The common observation, "I know what I want to say, I'm just having trouble getting it down on paper," is a half-truth at best. Getting words on paper almost always alters your ideas, and leads you to discover thoughts you didn't know you had. If you expect to have all the answers before you begin to write, you are more likely to settle for relatively superficial ideas. And, when you try to conduct all of your thinking in your head, you may arrive at an idea, but not be able to explain to your readers how you got there.

When you make the shift from freewriting to writing a first draft, you may not—and most likely will not—have all of the answers, but you will waste significantly less time chasing ill-focused and inadequately considered ideas than might otherwise have been the case.

The Rules for Freewriting There aren't many rules to freewriting.

The first is: pick a concrete starting point. Find *something specific* to be interested in. Notice & Focus works well for locating that focus as do "interesting" and "strange."

Write your focus at the top of the page—a few lines or a short list of details or a short passage. Then launch the freewrite from there.

Commit to an allotted time in which you will write continuously. Ten minutes is a minimum. You may be surprised at how much you can find to say in this amount of time. The more you do freewriting, the better you will get at it, and the longer you will be able to go.

Most importantly, keep your pen (or fingers on the keyboard) moving. Don't reread as you go. Don't pause to correct things. Don't cross things out. Don't quit when you think you have run out of things to say. Just keep writing.

Move 3: Make the Implicit Explicit. Push Observations to Implications by Asking "So What?"

NOTICE & FOCUS, "interesting" and "strange," as well as freewriting—these moves aim to keep writers dwelling longer in the observation phase of analysis, to spend more time exploring and amassing data before they leap to making some kind of claim. It's time now to shift our focus to the leap, itself.

One of the central activities and goals of analysis is to make explicit (overtly stated) what is implicit (suggested). When we do so, we are addressing such questions as "What follows from this?" and "If this is true, what else is true?" The pursuit of such questions—drawing out implications—moves our thinking and our writing *forward*.

MOVING FORWARD

Observation ⟶ So what? ⟶ Implications
Implications ⟶ So what? ⟶ Conclusions

© Cengage Learning®

This process of converting suggestions into direct statements is essential to analysis, but it is also the feature of analyzing that, among beginning writers, is least well understood. The fear is that, like the emperor's new clothes, implications aren't really "there," but are instead the phantasms of an overactive imagination. "Reading between the lines" is the common and telling phrase that expresses this anxiety. Throughout this book we will have more to say about the charge that analysis makes something out of nothing—the spaces between the lines rather than what is there in black and white. But for now, let's look at a hypothetical example of this process of drawing out implications, to suggest not only how it's done, but how often we do it in our everyday lives.

Imagine that you are driving down the highway and find yourself analyzing a billboard advertisement for a particular brand of beer. Such an analysis might begin with your noticing what the billboard photo contains, its various "parts"—six young, athletic-looking and scantily clad men and women drinking beer while pushing kayaks into a fast-running river. If you were to stop at this point, you would have produced not an analysis but a summary—a description of what the photo contains. If, however, you went on to consider what the particulars of the photo imply, your summary would become more analytical.

You might say, for example, that the photo implies that beer is the beverage of fashionable, healthy, active people, not just of older men with large stomachs dozing in armchairs in front of the television. Thus, the advertisement's meaning goes beyond its explicit contents; your analysis would lead you to convert to direct statement meanings that are suggested but not overtly stated, such as the advertisement's goal of attacking a common, negative stereotype about its product (that only fat, lazy, male people drink beer).The naming of parts that you do in analysis is not an end unto itself, is not an exercise in making something out of nothing; it serves the purpose of allowing you to better understand the nature of your subject. The implications of the "parts" you name are an important part of that understanding.

The word *implication* comes from the Latin *implicare*, which means "to fold in." The word *explicit* is in opposition to the idea of implication. It means "folded out." An act of mind is required to take what is folded in and to fold it out for all to see. This process of drawing out implications is also known as making inferences. *Inference* and *implication* are related but not synonymous

PUSHING OBSERVATIONS TO CONCLUSIONS: ASKING SO WHAT?

(shorthand for)

What does the observation imply?

Why does this observation matter?

Where does this observation get us?

How can we begin to theorize the significance of the observation?

© Cengage Learning®

---

terms. The term *implication* describes something suggested by the material itself; implications reside in the matter you are studying. The term *inference* describes your thinking process. In short, you infer what the subject implies.

ASKING "SO WHAT?"

ASKING "SO WHAT?" is a universal prompt for spurring the move from observation to implication and ultimately to interpretation. ASKING "SO WHAT?"—or its milder cousin, "And so?"—is a calling to account, a way of pressing yourself to confront that essential question, "Why does this matter?" The tone of "So what?" can sound rude or at least brusque, but that directness can be liberating. Often writers will go to great lengths to avoid stating what they take something to mean. After all, that leaves them open to attack, they fear, if they get it wrong. But ASKING "SO WHAT?" is a way of forcing yourself to take the plunge without too much hoopla. And when you are tempted to stop thinking too soon, ASKING "SO WHAT?" will press you onward.

ASKING "SO WHAT?" in a Chain

Experienced analytical writers develop the habit of "ASKING SO WHAT?" repeatedly. That is, they ask "So what?," answer, and then ask "So what?" of that answer, and often keep going (see Figure 4.2). The repeated asking of this question causes writers to move beyond their first attempt to arrive at a claim.

By sustaining their pursuit of implications, seasoned writers habitually reason in a chain rather than settling prematurely for a single link, as the next example illustrates.

The following is the opening paragraph of a talk given by a professor of Political Science at our college, Dr. Jack Gambino, on the occasion of a gallery

1 Describe significant evidence

2 Begin to query your own observations by making what is implicit explicit

3 Push your observations and statements of implications to interpretive conclusions by *again* asking So What?

© 2015 Cengage Learning®

FIGURE 4.2
ASKING "SO WHAT?"

opening featuring the work of two contemporary photographers of urban and industrial landscapes. We have located in brackets our annotations of his turns of thought, as these pivot on "strange" and "So what?" (Note: images referred to in the example are available from Google Images—type in Camilo Vergara fern street 1988, also Edward Burtynsky.)

If you look closely at Camilo Vergara's photo of Fern Street, Camden, 1988, you'll notice a sign on the side of a dilapidated building:

Danger: Men Working

W. Hargrove Demolition

Perhaps that warning captures the ominous atmosphere of these very different kinds of photographic documents by Camilo Vergara and Edward Burtynsky: "Danger: Men Working." Watch out—human beings are at work! But the work that is presented is not so much a building-up as it is a tearing-down—the work of demolition. **[strange: tearing down is unexpected; writer asks "So what?" and answers]**

Of course, demolition is often necessary in order to construct anew: old buildings are leveled for new projects, whether you are building a highway or bridge in an American city or a dam in the Chinese countryside. You might call modernity itself, as so many have, a process of creative destruction, a term used variously to describe modern art, capitalism, and technological innovation. The photographs in this exhibit, however, force us to pay attention to the "destructive" side of this modern equation. **[strange: photos emphasize destruction and not creation; writer asks "So what?" and answers]**

What both Burtynsky and Vergara do in their respective ways is to put up a warning sign—they question whether the reworking of our natural and social environment leads to a sustainable human future. And they wonder whether the process of creative destruction may not have spun recklessly out of control, producing places that are neither habitable nor sustainable. In fact, a common element connecting the two photographic versions is the near absence of people in the landscape. **[writer points to supporting feature of evidence, about which he will further theorize]**

While we see the evidence of the transforming power of human production on the physical and social environment, neither Vergara's urban ruins nor Burtynsky's industrial sites actually show us "men working." **[writer continues to move by noticing strange absence of people in photographs of sites where men work]** Isolated figures peer suspiciously out back doors or pick through the rubble, but they appear out of place. **[writer asks a final "So what?" and arrives at a conclusion:]** It is this sense of displacement— of human beings alienated from the environments they themselves have created—that provides the most haunting aspect of the work of these two photographers.

The Gambino opening is a good example of how ASKING "SO WHAT?" generates forward momentum for the analysis. Notice the pattern by which the paragraph moves: the observation of something strange, about which the writer asks and answers "So what?" several times until arriving at a final "So what?"—the point at which he decides what his observations ultimately mean. We call the final "So what?" in this chain of thinking the ultimate "So what?" because it moves from implications to the writer's culminating point.

Move 4: Look for Patterns of Repetition and Contrast and for Anomalies (THE METHOD)

We have been defining analysis as the understanding of parts in relation to each other and to a whole. But how do you know which parts to attend to? What makes some details in the material you are studying more worthy of your attention than others?

The procedure we call THE METHOD offers a tool for uncovering significant patterns. Like NOTICE AND FOCUS, THE METHOD orients you toward significant detail; but whereas NOTICE AND FOCUS is a deliberately unstructured activity, THE METHOD applies a matrix or grid of observational moves to a subject. In its most reduced form, THE METHOD organizes observation and then prompts interpretation by asking the following sequence of questions.

In virtually all subjects, repetition and close resemblance (strands) are signs of emphasis. In a symphony, for example, certain patterns of notes repeat throughout, announcing themselves as major themes. In Shakespeare's play *King Lear*, references to seeing and eyes call attention to themselves through repetition, causing us to recognize that the play is <u>about</u> seeing. Binary oppositions, which often consist of two strands or repetitions that are in tension with each other, suggest what is at stake in a subject. We can understand *King Lear* by the way it opposes kinds of blindness to ways of seeing.

Along with looking for pattern, it is also fruitful to attend to anomalous details—those that seem not to fit the pattern. Anomalies help us to revise our assumptions. Picture, for example, a TV ad featuring a baseball player reading Dostoyevsky in the dugout. In this case, the anomaly, a baseball player who reads serious literature, subverts the stereotypical assumption that sports and intellectualism don't belong together.

QUESTIONS FROM THE METHOD

What repeats?

What goes with what? (strands)

What is opposed to what? (binaries)

(for all of these) $\longrightarrow$ SO WHAT?

What doesn't fit? (anomalies) So what?

People tend to avoid information that challenges (by not conforming to) views they already hold. Screening out anything that would ruffle the pattern they've begun to see, they ignore the evidence that might lead them to a better theory. Most advances in thought have arisen when someone has observed some phenomenon that does not fit within a prevailing theory.

The Steps of THE METHOD

THE METHOD of looking for patterns works through a series of steps. Hold yourself initially to doing the steps one at a time and in order. Later, you will be able to record your answers under each of the five steps simultaneously. Although the steps of THE METHOD are discrete and modular, they are also consecutive. They proceed by a kind of narrative logic. Each step leads logically to the next, and then to various kinds of regrouping, which is actually rethinking (see Figure 4.3).

1 **List exact repetitions and the number of each (words, details).** For example, if forms of the word *seems* repeat three times, write "seems × 3." With images, the repeated appearance of high foreheads would constitute an exact repetition. Concentrate on substantive (meaning-carrying) words. Only in rare cases will words like "and" or "the" merit attention as a significant repetition. At the most literal level, whatever repeats is what the thing is about.

2 **List repetitions of the same or similar kind of detail or word—which we call strands** (for example, *polite, courteous, decorous*). Be able to explain the strand's connecting logic with a label: *manners*.

3 **List details or words that form or suggest binary oppositions**—pairs of words or details that are opposites—and select from these the most important ones, which function as **organizing contrasts** (for example, *open/closed, ugly/beautiful, global/local*). Your goal here is not to engage in either/or thinking but to locate what is at stake in the subject, the tensions and issues that it is trying to resolve.

4 **Choose ONE repetition, strand, or binary as a starting point for a healthy paragraph** (or two) in which you discuss its significance in relation to the whole. (This ranking, as in Notice and Focus, prompts an interpretive leap.)

5 **Locate anomalies: exceptions to the pattern, things that seem not to fit.** Once you see an anomaly, you will often find that it is part of a strand you had not detected (and perhaps one side of a previously unseen binary).

FIGURE 4.3

THE METHOD

Expect ideas to suggest themselves to you as you move through the steps of THE METHOD. Strands often begin to suggest other strands that are in opposition to them. Words you first took to be parts of one strand may migrate to different strands. This process of noticing and then relocating words and details into different patterns is one aspect of doing THE METHOD that can push your analysis to interpretation.

It may be helpful to think of this method of analysis as a form of mental doodling. Rather than worrying about what you are going to say, or about whether or not you understand, you instead get out a pencil and start tallying up what you see. Engaged in this process, you'll soon find yourself gaining entry to the logic of your subject matter.

Two Examples of THE METHOD Generating Ideas

In the paragraph below you can see how the writer's noticing strands and binaries directs his thinking.

> The most striking aspect of the spots is how different they are from typical fashion advertising. If you look at men's fashion magazines, for example, at the advertisements for the suits of Ralph Lauren or Valentino or Hugo Boss, they almost always consist of a beautiful man, with something interesting done to his hair, wearing a gorgeous outfit. At the most, the man may be gesturing discreetly, or smiling in the demure way that a man like that might smile after, say, telling the supermodel at the next table no thanks he has to catch an early-morning flight to Milan. But that's all. The beautiful face and the clothes tell the whole story. The Dockers ads, though, are almost exactly the opposite. There's no face. The camera is jumping around so much that it's tough to concentrate on the clothes. And instead of stark simplicity, the fashion image is overlaid with a constant, confusing pattern. It's almost as if the Dockers ads weren't primarily concerned with clothes at all—and in fact that's exactly what Levi's intended. What the company had discovered, in its research, was that baby-boomer men felt that the chief thing missing from their lives was male friendship. Caught between the demands of the families that many of them had started in the eighties and career considerations that had grown more onerous, they felt they had lost touch with other men. The purpose of the ads—the chatter, the lounging around, the quick cuts—was simply to conjure up a place where men could put on one-hundred-percent-cotton khakis and reconnect with one another. In the original advertising brief, that imaginary place was dubbed Dockers World.
>
> — MALCOLM GLADWELL, "LISTENING TO KHAKIS"

First Gladwell notes the differences in two kinds of fashion ads aimed at men. There are the high fashion ads and the Dockers ads. In the first of these, the word "beautiful" repeats twice as part of a strand (including "gorgeous," "interesting," "supermodel," "demure"). The writer then poses traits of the Dockers ads as an opposing strand. Instead of a beautiful face there is no face; instead of "gorgeous outfit," "it's tough to concentrate on the clothes." These oppositions cause the writer to make his interpretive leap, that the Dockers ads "weren't primarily concerned with clothes at all" and that this was intentional.

In the student essay, below, Lesley Stephen develops a key contrast between two thinkers, Sigmund Freud and Michel Foucault, by noticing the different meanings that each attaches to some of the same key words. THE METHOD helps to locate the key terms and to define them by seeing what other words they suggest (strands).

> Freud defines civilization as serving two main purposes. The first is to protect men against nature, and the second is to adjust their mutual relations. Freud seems to offer returning to nature as a possible solution for men's sexual freedom. I think Freud might

believe that returning to nature by rejecting civilization could bring about sexual freedom, but that sexual freedom does not necessarily equal happiness.

Foucault completely defies Freud's idea that sexuality is natural and that repression exists as anti-sexuality. He believes that everything is created from discourse; nothing is natural. And because nothing is natural, nothing is repressed. There is no such thing as a natural desire; if the desire exists, it is because it is already part of the discourse.

By focusing on repetitions of the words "nature" and "natural" and then seeing what goes with what, the writer creates a succinct and revealing comparison.

Doing The Method on a Poem

Here is an example of how one might do THE METHOD on a piece of text—in this case—a student poem. We use a poem because it is compact and so allows us to illustrate efficiently how THE METHOD works.

> Brooklyn Heights, 4:00 A.M.
> Dana Ferrelli
>
> sipping a warm forty oz.
>
> Coors Light on a stoop in
>
> Brooklyn Heights. I look
>
> across the street, in the open window;
>
> Blonde bobbing heads, the
>
> smack of a jump rope, laughter
>
> of my friends breaking
>
> beer bottles. Putting out their
>
> burning filters on the #5 of
>
> a hopscotch court.
>
> We reminisce of days when we were
>
> Fat, pimple faced—
>
> look how far we've come. But tomorrow
>
> a little blonde girl will
>
> pick up a Marlboro Light filter, just to play.
>
> And I'll buy another forty, because
>
> that's how I play now.
>
> Reminiscing about how far I've come

Here are the steps of THE METHOD, applied to the preceding poem.

1. *Words that repeat exactly:* forty × 2, blonde × 2, how far we've (I've) come × 2, light × 2, reminisce, reminiscing × 2, filter, filters × 2, Brooklyn Heights × 2

2. *Strands*: jump rope, laughter, play, hopscotch (connecting logic: childhood games, the carefree worldview of childhood), Coors Light, Marlboro Light filters, beer bottles (connecting logic: drugs, adult "games," escapism?),

   Smack, burning, breaking (connecting logic: violent actions and powerful emotion: burning)

3. *Binary oppositions*: how far we've come/how far I've come (a move from plural to singular, from a sense of group identity to isolation, from group values to a more individual consideration)

   Burning/putting out

   Coors Light, Marlboro Lights/jump rope, hopscotch

   How far I've come (two meanings of *far?*, one positive, one not)

   Heights/stoop

   Present/past

4. *Ranked repetitions, strands and binaries plus paragraph explaining the choice of one of these as central to understanding.*

   Most important repetitions: forty, how far we've/I've come

   Most important strands: childhood games and adulthood games

   Most important binaries: Burning versus putting out, open and laughter versus putting out

5. *Anomaly*: Fat, pimple faced—

   This detail does not fit with the otherwise halcyon treatment of childhood.

ANALYSIS (HEALTHY PARAGRAPHS) The repetition of *forty* (forty ounce beer) is interesting. It signals a certain weariness—perhaps with a kind of pun on *forty* to suggest middle age and thus the speaker's concern about moving toward being older in a way that seems stale and flat. The beer, after all, is warm—which is not the best state for a beer to be in, once opened, if it is to retain its taste and character. Forty ounces of beer might also suggest excess—"supersizing."

The most important (or at least most interesting) binary opposition is *burning versus putting out*. This binary seems to be part of a more intense strand in the poem, one that runs counter to the weary prospect of moving on toward a perhaps lonely ("how far *I've* come") middle-aged feeling. Burning goes with breaking and the smack of the jump rope, and even putting out (a strand), if we visualize putting out not just as fire extinguished but in terms of putting a cigarette out by pushing the burning end of it into something (the number 5 on the Hopscotch court). The poem's language has a violent and passionate edge to it, even though the violent words are not always in a violent context (for example, the smack of the jump rope).

This is a rather melancholy poem in which, perhaps, the speaker is mourning the passing, the "putting out" of the passion of youth ("burning"). In the poem's more obvious binary—the opposition of childhood games to more "adult" ones—the same melancholy plays itself out, making the poem's refrain-like repetition of "how far I've come" ring with unhappy irony. The little blonde girl is an image of the speaker's own past self (since the poem talks about reminiscing), and the speaker mourns that little girl's (her own) passing into a more uncertain and less carefree state. It is 4:00 A.M. in Brooklyn Heights—just about the end of night, the darkest point perhaps before the beginning of morning. But windows are open, suggesting possibility, so things are not all bad. The friends make noise together, break bottles together, revisit hopscotch square 5 together, and contemplate moving on.

Note: the reference to "Fat, pimple faced—" in the poem is an anomaly in the otherwise idealized representation of childhood in terms of games and laughter. The young women in the poem are sad that they can re-enact childhood games but they can't recover childhood's innocent happiness. The anomaly usefully reminds us of adults' desire to idealize the past by forgetting that the past has pimples as well as hopscotch. "Fat, pimple faced—" goes with what we might also be able to see as an anomaly—the open windows in what the poem otherwise describes as a steady closing down of hope.

Notice how this discussion moves from analysis of a key repetition and a key binary to a series of claims about the meaning of the poem as a whole. Writing about the data that THE METHOD has gathered leads us to see how the significant parts are related (Move 2 of the Five Analytical Moves).

Troubleshooting THE METHOD

THE METHOD is a means to an end, not an end in itself. Deciding what goes with what is an analytical move. It's not just listing. One aim of THE METHOD is to induce you to pay more attention, and a different kind of attention, to what you are studying.

Don't let the procedure turn into tedious or superficial data-gathering. Look for the *interesting* repetitions, strands and binaries, not just the most prevalent ones. Let this activity generate ideas.

In applying THE METHOD to longer texts, don't try to cover everything, and don't start making your lists until you have done a chunk of the reading. After all, you can't be expected to recognize a repetition in an extended essay until it has reappeared several times. Keep informal lists in the margins as you read, or in the inside cover of a book. When you become aware of an opposition, you can mark it with a +/− next to the paragraph where you were struck.

THE METHOD is designed to prompt thinking. You should be able to offer your reasons for why you think a given repetition or strand is most important. You should be able to express what issue you think is at stake in the organizing contrast you choose as most important.

As you look over your binaries, choose the binary that you think organizes the thinking in the subject as a whole—the *organizing* contrast. Which binary contains, implicitly or explicitly, the central issue or question or problem that is being addressed?

To make THE METHOD spark ideas, remember to ask So what? as a way of moving from observation to implication.

Move 5: Keep Reformulating Questions and Explanations

The preceding four analytical moves can be thought of in question form. The process of posing and answering such questions—the analytical process—is one of trial and error. Learning to write well is largely a matter of learning how to frame questions. Whatever questions you ask, the answers you propose won't always turn out to be answers, but may, instead, produce more questions. It follows that you need to keep the process of understanding open, often longer than feels comfortable. You do so by repeatedly reformulating your questions and explanations and going back to the original data for nourishment.

The following three groups of questions (organized according to the analytical moves they're derived from) are typical of what goes on in an analytical writer's head as he or she attempts to understand a subject. These questions will work with almost anything that you want to think about. As you will see, the questions are geared toward helping you locate and try on explanations for the meaning of various patterns of details.

> Which details seem significant? Why?
> What does the detail mean?
> What else might it mean?
>> (Moves: Define Significant Parts; Make the Implicit Explicit)
> How do the details fit together? What do they have in common?
> What does this pattern of details mean?
> What else might this same pattern of details mean? How else could
>> it be explained?
>> (Move: Look for Patterns)
> What details don't seem to fit? How might they be connected with other
>> details to form a different pattern?
> What does this new pattern mean? How might it cause me to read the
>> meaning of individual details differently?
>> (Moves: Look for Anomalies and Keep Asking Questions)

We conclude this chapter with an analysis of a famous painting that has come to be known as *Whistler's Mother*.

Summing Up: Analyzing *Whistler's Mother*

Throughout the chapter we have emphasized the importance of slowing down leaps to conclusions in order to spend more time dwelling with the data, carefully describing what you notice. We have stressed the importance of focusing on the details, looking for questions rather than answers, and telling yourself you don't understand even when you think you might. We've also said that summary and description are close cousins of and necessary to analysis, but that analysis provides more interpretive thinking—making the implicit explicit.

Key to any kind of analysis is laying out the data, not simply because it keeps the analysis accurate, but also because, crucially, it is in the act of carefully describing a subject that analytical writers often have their best ideas. What might an analysis of Whistler's painting include and why? (see Figure 4.4).

The first step is to describe with care. Look for the painting's significant parts and how they're related (Move 2) and for patterns of repetition and contrast (Move 4). The words you choose to describe your data will contain the germs of your ideas about what the subject means. In moving from description to analysis, scrutinize the language you have chosen, asking, "Why did I choose this word?" and "What ideas are implicit in the language I have used?" This attention to your own language will help you to make the implicit explicit (Move 3).

RMN-Grand Palais/Art Resource, NY

FIGURE 4.4

Arrangement In Grey and Black: The Artist's Mother by James Abbott McNeill Whistler, 1871

Data	Analytical Moves	Interpretive Leaps (So What?)
subject in profile, not looking at us	make implicit explicit (speculate about what the detail might suggest)	figure strikes us as separate, nonconfrontational, passive
folded hands, fitted lace cap, contained hair, expressionless face	locate pattern of same or similar detail; make what is implicit in pattern of details explicit	figure strikes us as self-contained, powerful in her separateness and self-enclosure— self-sufficient?
patterned curtain and picture versus still figure and blank wall; slightly frilled lace cuffs and ties on cap versus plain black dress	locate organizing contrast; make what is implicit in the contrast explicit	austerity and containment of the figure made more pronounced by slight contrast with busier, more lively, and more ornate elements and with little picture showing world outside
slightly slouched body position and presence of support for feet	anomalies; make what is implicit in the anomalies explicit	these details destabilize the serenity of the figure, adding some tension to the picture in the form of slightly uneasy posture and figure's need for support: she looks too long, drooped in on her own spine

© Cengage Learning®

FIGURE 4.5

Summary and Analysis of WHISTLER'S MOTHER Diagram

Figure 4.5 is a depiction of this analytical process in outline form.

What does this analysis tell us? It might tell us that the painter's choice to portray his subject in profile contributes to our sense of her separateness from us and of her nonconfrontational passivity. We look at her, but she does not look back at us. Her black dress and the fitted lace cap that obscures her hair are not only emblems of her self-effacement, shrouds disguising her identity like her expressionless face, but also the tools of her self-containment and thus of her power to remain aloof from prying eyes.

What is the attraction of this painting (this being one of the questions that an analysis might ask)? What might draw a viewer to the sight of this austere, drably attired woman, sitting alone in the center of a mostly blank space? Perhaps it is the very starkness of the painting, and the mystery of self-sufficiency at its center, that attracts us.

You may not agree with the terms by which we have summarized the painting, and thus you may not agree with such conclusions as "the mystery of self-sufficiency." Nor is it necessary that you agree, because there is no single, right answer to what the painting means. But the process of careful observation and description and repeated tries at interpretation by ASKING SO WHAT? has produced claims about what and how the painting communicates that others would at least find reasonable and fair.

Analysis and Personal Associations

Although observations like those offered in the "Interpretive Leaps" column in Figure 4.5 go beyond simple description, they stay with the task of explaining the painting, rather than moving to private associations that the painting might prompt, such as effusions about old age or rocking chairs or the character and situation of the writer's own mother. Such associations could well be valuable unto themselves as a means of prompting a searching piece of expressive writing. They might also help a writer to interpret some feature of the painting that he or she was working to understand. But the writer would not be free to use pieces of his or her personal history as conclusions about what the painting communicates, unless these conclusions could also be reasonably inferred from the painting itself.

Analysis is a creative activity, a fairly open form of inquiry, but its imaginative scope is governed by logic. The hypothetical analysis we have offered is not the only reading of the painting that a viewer might make, because the same pattern of details might lead to different conclusions. But a viewer would not be free to conclude anything he or she wished, such as that the woman is mourning the death of a son or is patiently waiting to die. Such conclusions would be unfounded speculations, since the black dress is not sufficient to support them. Analysis often operates in areas where there is no one right answer, but like summary and argument, it requires the writer to reason from evidence.

CHAPTER 5

What Are Secondary Sources, and Why Do You Need Them?

In order to successfully complete the Analytical Research Project, you will need to make use of two very different kinds of sources: a primary source and several secondary sources. Your primary source—the artifact that you are analyzing for your research paper—has a central and basic role in the project. As we have previously discussed, you will be making an argument about your primary source. The role of secondary sources is more complex and challenging to master.

As we discussed in Chapter One, secondary sources are written texts such as academic papers, magazine or newspaper articles, essays, or chapters from books that examine objects, data, or phenomena and make analytical claims about them. These sources are *secondary* in that they are not the primary focus of your analytical argument. Instead, they are sources that you will draw upon to develop stronger, more complex, and better-supported ideas about your primary source.

Why Are Secondary Sources Important?

By using secondary sources in your work, you draw upon the knowledge, insight, and accumulated ideas of an intellectual community that is much larger than yourself. No scholar is in a position to be an expert on everything. Instead, scholars continually rely upon, challenge, and critique each other's work.

The Analytical Research Project offers you an opportunity to participate in the life and conversation of this intellectual community. Participating successfully in this conversation requires understanding what has already been said, both so that you will not simply repeat ideas, and so that you can build on other people's contributions.

Think of your own experience with conversations at parties. If you approach a group of people and simply begin talking about your own ideas and experiences, you might seem rude or eccentric. It's likely that you would listen to the conversation first, so that you can find a way to intervene. You might say, for instance: "It's interesting that you say that, because I've found…" "I agree, and I can think of another example," or: "Actually, I think that the opposite is true."

In this case, the new ideas that you are offering will be about your primary source. However, they will also form a part of larger ongoing conversations about topics relevant to that primary source, which might include, for instance, advertising, music, gender, race, politics, or identity.

Despite the fact that you, as an undergraduate student, may not (and, indeed, almost certainly will not) be familiar with the full scope of the intellectual conversation happening around these issues, drawing on the work of other writers allows you to make a thoughtful, insightful, and potentially valuable contribution—particularly as it is unlikely that any writer has ever analyzed the rhetoric of your specific primary source.

You might see that this suggests another reason why secondary sources are important: by using these sources skillfully, you assure your reader that you are familiar with key elements of the intellectual conversation about the topics you are discussing. Your use of these sources contributes to the construction of a strong *ethos*, and can help you to persuade your reader to accept your argument. In order for this tactic to succeed, you will need to carefully consider which sources you use, and how you use them.

How to Find and Choose Secondary Sources

Your English 1110 teacher will introduce you to the library resources that you will use to search for secondary sources. However, there is more involved in finding and choosing sources than simply accessing the right database or going to the library. You will need to understand how to appropriately focus your search and how to evaluate the credibility of the authors and sources you find.

The basis of successful research is a clearly articulated research question— in other words, a question that points you towards the area in your primary source that you find most interesting, strange, or significant. This will not be a question that you can answer by locating a fact (such as a name, date, or measurement), but rather a question that you will seek to answer by constructing a well-supported argument. The function of research questions is, in many ways, similar to that of a funnel or a sieve for information: if they are too narrow, *no* useful information will get through—but if they are too broad, the information that gets through will be all shapes and sizes, and you will not have successfully sifted out the information that is most useful to you.

Example: Research Questions

For a student writing a paper about the Apple advertisement on page [34], examples of strong research questions might be:

- What characteristics of Benjamin Franklin might lead Apple to use him as a figure in computer advertisements?
- What role did gender play in early computer advertisements?
- Why does an advertisement for new technology place its technology in a scene from the eighteenth-century American Revolution?

Less effective research questions might be:

- Who was Benjamin Franklin? (This question is very broad, and much of the research involved in answering it will not help you to understand why Apple might have included Benjamin Franklin in its advertisement.)

- What types of computers did Apple sell in 1980? (This is a narrow factual question, not a question that requires interpretation or argument as an answer.)

- How successful was this advertising campaign? (Again, this is a factual question. It also seems unlikely to point you towards research that will help you interpret or understand the text.)

The goal of your research will be to uncover sources that will help you to construct your argument. These sources will not always be sources that agree with your instincts or ideas. They may be sources that challenge your instincts and ideas, or with which you find you disagree. It is important to remember that the most valuable sources are often those that pose interesting challenges to your own way of thinking.

Secondary sources may also be primarily concerned with topics that at first seem different to your own. Just as you have a primary source that forms the basis of your research paper, other authors have texts on which their articles are focused. These texts may not be connected to your own primary source. This does not mean that the articles in question are not valuable secondary sources! For instance, if you are researching the depiction of robots in modern movies, you may find a number of articles about the 1982 science fiction film *Blade Runner*. Even if your primary source is not connected to *Blade Runner* (let's say you have chosen a poster for the 2004 film *I, Robot*), it's possible that one or more of these articles might offer helpful insight about the depiction of robots in film.

In fact, it may sometimes be useful for you to consider other examples of texts similar to your primary source (possibly in a variety of media) and search for articles about these similar texts. If your primary source uses images or language from fairy tales, you might search for articles that have been written about movies based on fairy tales. If your primary source features images of natural disaster, you might search for articles that have been written about disaster movies. Often, these articles will contain insights that are applicable on a broader level, and they may cause you to see your primary source in a new light.

Once you have located articles that seem to be relevant to your interests, your next task will be to evaluate their credibility as sources. In other words, what establishes this article as a believable source of information? How do you know that you can trust the author or the publisher of the article?

When evaluating credibility, there are several factors that you should take into consideration:

Where has the Article Been Published? A credible article will generally be published by a journal, magazine, or newspaper that has a strong reputation. This might be the print or online version of a well-established newspaper such as the *New York Times*, a highly-regarded magazine/website such as *The Atlantic*, a digital film and television site such as *The A.V. Club*, or a peer-reviewed academic journal published by a university, such as The Ohio State University's *Disability Studies Quarterly*. Understanding who is publishing the article will help you make an informed decision about that article's trustworthiness.

What are the Author's Credentials? Who is the author of the article, and what qualifies that author to write on this topic? An author's credentials (the characteristics that qualify the author to write about a particular topic) are a part of the author's ethos. It may be that the author in question is a professor at a top university (a professor at The Ohio State University, even!) who has spent years investigating the topic. The author might also be an award-winning journalist who has written extensively on similar issues. You would probably be inclined to trust authors such as these. However, if the author of the article does not appear to have any relevant credentials, this might cause you to question that author's credibility. You might also question an author's credibility if you discovered an article about quantum physics had been written by a chef, or that an article about fine cooking had been written by a quantum physicist. There might be a perfectly good reason for these authors to be writing outside of their area of expertise, but at the very least, you would want to investigate them further.

What Are an Author's or Publisher's Biases? When writing a researched paper, you have a responsibility to recognize the assumptions and biases that different authors bring to their writing. For example, Fox News generally has a conservative bias in its reporting, whereas MSNBC generally has a liberal one. These examples are fairly obvious and easy to spot, but in fact all writers make assumptions and bring their own preconceptions to their work, sometimes in subtle ways. Bias does not mean that an article cannot be a valuable source—in fact, there are times when you may wish to discuss a particular opinion or worldview—however, the question of bias is a significant one to keep in mind when you are deciding how and whether an article might be useful. For instance, you might suspect that an article about the future of robotics written by the CEO of a robotics corporation is somewhat biased. Similarly, an article about a government's foreign policy written by a senior member of that government is probably not going to take a neutral view.

How Effective is the Author's Ethos? As part of your rhetorical education, you are learning the techniques that allow you to build a persuasive *ethos*. You may also begin to recognize the signs or absences of these techniques in other authors. If an author makes frequent, obvious spelling or grammatical errors in a published work, this might cause you to question that author's credibility or provide some warning that the work has not been thoroughly reviewed for professional publication. Similarly, if an author makes repeated factual errors, you might question how knowledgeable that author really is.

Assessing these factors together should allow you to make thoughtful decisions about the credibility of articles, which in turn should allow you to make thoughtful decisions about which articles will prove most valuable as secondary sources.

How to Use Secondary Sources

Many students believe that using a secondary source is as simple as locating a sentence that seems to agree with their argument, putting it into a paper, and placing quotation marks on either side of it. It is common for students to state a claim, then use this type of quotation from a secondary source to "prove" that the claim is correct. While it's true that secondary sources can provide *evidence* to support a claim, you should remember that the types of claims you are making in your Analytical Research Paper are generally claims that cannot be proven or disproven in this manner. Instead, you will persuade your audience of their merit through strong and well-supported arguments.

Secondary sources are a vital part of constructing this kind of argument. However, to use them effectively, you must do more than simply mine them for quotations. The key point to consider when you are working with secondary sources is: **What is this secondary source contributing to your argument?** The foundation of any work you do with a secondary source should be a way in which that source makes an important contribution to your argument. In other words, you should not use a source simply because it sounds impressive or was the easiest to find. You should be able to explain (to yourself and, when necessary, to your teacher—for example, in the Annotated Bibliography) why you feel it is important to use this particular source. Once you have located the key contribution that a source is making to your argument, you can begin to consider which specific parts of that source you wish to quote or paraphrase in your research paper.

There are many different kinds of contributions that a secondary source can make to your argument. A secondary source might **support** your argument by providing an example that illustrates a point that you are making. It might **establish** the point in the intellectual conversation at which you wish to intervene. (Think about our example of the party conversation: a common way to enter a conversation is to say, "It's interesting that you say that, because I think...") A secondary source might **challenge** your argument by raising points that you wish to critique or argue against. It might raise **new ideas** or **questions** that you wish to explore in your research paper. It might serve as a **lens** (like a magnifying glass or a prism) through which you can see your primary source in new and interesting ways.

Here are some tips for using secondary sources effectively:

Paraphrase Paraphrasing literally means "saying the same thing in different words." Paraphrasing sentences or arguments from a secondary source (rather than simply quoting them) can be a valuable tool for you. Firstly, it requires you to fully understand all the nuances of a secondary source's language—something that is absolutely essential when you are using a source. Secondly, it allows you to highlight for your audience the exact elements of your source that you find important. In a sense, you are interpreting your source for your audience. It is important to remember that if you are directly paraphrasing a source, you should still include a citation.

Continue the Conversation Remember that you are taking part in an active and ongoing discussion. This makes you an *interlocutor*—a word used to describe someone who is involved in a conversation, but which literally means "someone who speaks among or between." As an interlocutor, you want to keep the conversation going. This may mean questioning, challenging, or criticizing your sources, just as you might question, challenge, or criticize other members of a conversation. It might also mean pointing out ways in which sources challenge or criticize each other. What you should *not* do is let the conversation die by simply agreeing or disagreeing with a source and letting this be the last word.

Don't Think in Binaries Not only is it okay to agree with some parts of a source and disagree with other parts of a source, this is important and valuable. If you judge potential sources simply as "good" or "bad," "right" or "wrong," you are preventing yourself from seeing the rich and interesting contributions that get hidden by these labels. Instead, embrace the tensions and contradictions of sources, and allow yourself to question and critique these aspects.

Don't Forget Your Own Voice As the author of your research paper, you are using secondary sources as material with which to build a more solid argument. You might think of your sources as a kind of building material, which you will combine with others' materials and with your own to make an attractive, solidly constructed building. Your architectural design—your own voice and argument—should be what stands out. To this end, you should always consider how you are adding to or challenging what others have said. We began by asking what your sources were contributing to your argument. Make sure that you also understand what *you* are contributing to your argument!

Of course, it's not enough to just drop in quotations without context or transition; there are rules and customs for how to do so. To help you learn more about how to combine your words with other writers' words at a sentence level, we turn again to *Writing Analytically*.

Integrating Quotations Into Your Paper

An enormous number of writers lose authority and readability because they have never learned how to correctly integrate quotations into their own writing. The following guidelines should help. The primary rules of thumb here are that you should:

- Tell your readers in the text of your paper, not just in citations, when you are using someone else's words, ideas, or information; rewording someone else's idea doesn't make it your idea.

- Always attach a quotation to some of your own language; never let it stand as its own sentence in your text.

1. **Acknowledge sources in your text, not just in citations.** *When you incorporate material from a source, attribute it to the source explicitly in your text—not just in a citation.* In other words, when you introduce the material, *frame* it with a phrase such as "according to Marsh" or "as Gruen argues."

   Although it is not required, you are usually much better off making the attribution overtly, even if you have also cited the source within parentheses or with a footnote at the end of the last sentence quoted, paraphrased, or summarized. If a passage does not contain an attribution, your readers will not know that it comes from a source until they reach the citation at the end. Attributing up front clearly distinguishes what one source says from what another says and, perhaps more importantly, what your sources say from what you say. Useful verbs for introducing attributions include the following: notes, observes, argues, comments, writes, says, reports, suggests, and claims. Generally speaking, by the way, you should cite the author by last name only—as "Gruen," not as "William Gruen" or "Mr. Gruen." (In some cases, the first appearance includes both first and last name.)

2. **Splice quotations onto your own words.** *Always attach some of your own language to quotations; don't let them sit in your text as independent sentences with quotation marks around them.* You can normally satisfy this rule with an attributive phrase—commonly known as a tag phrase—that introduces the quotation.

   According to Paul McCartney, "All you need is love."

Note that the tag phrase takes a comma before the quote.

Alternatively you can splice quotations into your text with a setup: a statement followed by a colon.

   Patrick Henry's famous phrase is one of the first that American schoolchildren memorize: "Give me liberty, or give me death."

The colon, you should notice, usually comes at the end of an independent clause (that is, a subject plus verb that can stand alone), at the spot where a period normally goes. It would be incorrect to write "Patrick Henry is known for: 'Give me liberty, or give me death.'"

The rationale for this guideline on splicing in quotations is essentially the same as that for the previous one: if you are going to move to quotation, you first need to identify its author so that your readers will be able to put it in context quickly.

Spliced quotations frequently create problems in grammar or punctuation for writers. Whether you include an entire sentence (or passage) of quotation or just a few phrases, you need to take care to integrate them into the grammar of your own sentence.

One of the most common mistaken assumptions is that a comma should always precede a quotation, as in "A spokesperson for the public defender's office demanded, 'an immediate response from the mayor.'" The sentence structure does not call for any punctuation after "demanded."

3. **Cite sources after quotations.** *Locate citations in parentheses after the quotation and before the final period.* The information about the source appears at the end of the sentence, with the final period following the closing parenthesis.

> A recent article on the best-selling albums in America claimed that "Ever since Elvis, it has been pop music's job to challenge the mores of the older generation" (Hornby 168).

Note that there is normally *no punctuation* at the end of the quotation itself, either before or after the closing quotation mark. A quotation that ends either in a question mark or an exclamation mark is an exception to this rule because the sign is an integral part of the quotation's meaning.

> As Hamlet says to Rosencrantz and Guildenstern, "And yet to me what is this quintessence of dust?" (2.2.304–05).

4. **Use ellipses to shorten quotations.** *Add an ellipsis to indicate that you have omitted some of the language from within the quotation.* Form an ellipses by entering three dots (periods) with spaces in between them, or use four dots to indicate that the deletion continues to the end of the sentence (the last dot becomes the period). Suppose you wanted to shorten the following quotation from a recent article about Radiohead by Alex Ross:

> The album "OK Computer," with titles like "Paranoid Android," "Karma Police," and "Climbing Up the Walls," pictured the onslaught of the information age and a young person's panicky embrace of it (Ross 85).

Using an ellipsis, you could emphasize the source's claim by omitting the song titles from the middle of the sentence:

> The album "OK Computer"... pictured the onslaught of the information age and a young person's panicky embrace of it (Ross 85).

In most cases, the gap between quoted passages should be short, and in any case, you should be careful to preserve the sense of the original. The standard joke about ellipses is pertinent here: A reviewer writes that a film "will delight no one and appeal to the intelligence of invertebrates only, but not average viewers." An unethical advertiser cobbles together pieces of the review to say that the film "will delight... and appeal to the intelligence of... viewers."

5. **Use square brackets to alter or add information within a quotation.** Sometimes it is necessary to change the wording slightly inside a quotation to maintain fluency. Square brackets indicate that you are altering the original quotation. Brackets are also used when you insert explanatory information, such as a definition or example, within a quotation. Here are a few examples that alter the original quotations previously cited.

> According to one music critic, the cultural relevance of Radiohead is evident in "the album 'OK Computer'...[which] pictured the onslaught of the information age and a young person's panicky embrace of it" (Ross 85).

> Popular music has always "[challenged] the mores of the older generation," according to Nick Hornby (168).

Note that both examples respect the original sense of the quotation; they have changed the wording only to integrate the quotations gracefully within the writer's own sentence structure.

CHAPTER 6

Writing the Paper

Writing Rhetoric: The Goal of Your Paper

Thus far, your encounters with rhetoric have mostly taken place from the position of an analyst. That is: you have looked at rhetoric from the viewpoint of someone who is trying to understand how and why particular rhetorical choices have been made by the author of a text.

However, writing a research paper asks you to encounter rhetoric from another position: the position of an author. As the author of a paper, you will be employing rhetoric in order to persuade your audience to accept the claim that you are making—just as the authors of your primary source have employed rhetoric in order to convince their audience to accept a particular message.

It is important to remember that the choices you make in writing your research paper are rhetorical choices. Your *ethos* as an author may be enhanced or damaged by these choices—from your correct citation and integration of sources to your use of punctuation and grammar that meets the expectations of academic English. You are not merely fulfilling the rote demands of an assignment rubric. You are attempting to convince your audience of your competence as an author and thinker. This task—the task of communicating your ideas in a persuasive and compelling manner—is one that you will face in many forms throughout your academic career and beyond.

Carefully consider, therefore, how you can construct a paper that will best achieve your goals as an author. This means paying attention to every element of your paper, from its broad structure and organization to the more specific details of thesis statements, transitions, quotations, and style.

In this chapter, we offer a guide to some of the major issues you will consider while planning and writing your research paper.

What is the Substance of Your Paper?

As you already know, the topic of your Analytical Research Paper is your primary source. More specifically, the argument you are making in your Analytical Research Paper is an analytical argument about your primary source. All of the work you've done the Five Analytical Moves has given you a large amount of observations, and The Method has led you to begin making claims about all of this evidence. In order to construct an effective argument, you'll need to link your claims to appropriate evidence from your primary source and from your secondary sources. Here, *Writing Analytically* provides us good advice on how to actually do that.

Linking Evidence and Claims

The relationship between evidence and claims is rarely self-evident. The word *evident* comes from a Latin verb meaning "to see." To say that the truth of a statement is "self-evident" means that it does not need proving because its truth can be plainly seen by all. The thought connections that have occurred to you about what the evidence means will not automatically occur to others. Persuasive writing always makes the connections between evidence and claim overt (see Figure 6.1).

The first step in learning to explain the connection between your evidence and your claims is to remember that evidence rarely, if ever, can be left to speak for itself. When you leave evidence to speak for itself, you are assuming that it can be interpreted in only one way and that others will necessarily think as you do.

Writers who think that evidence speaks for itself generally do very little with it. Sometimes they will present it without making any overt claims, stating, for example, "There was no alcohol at the party," and expecting the reader to understand this statement as a sign of approval or disapproval. Alternatively, they may simply place the evidence next to a claim: "The party was terrible—there was no alcohol," or "The party was great—there was no alcohol." Juxtaposing the evidence with the claim (just putting them next to each other) leaves out the thinking that connects them, thereby implying that the logic of the connection is obvious. But even for readers prone to agreeing with a given claim, simply pointing to the evidence is rarely enough.

The Functions of Evidence

A common assumption about evidence is that it is "the stuff that proves I'm right." Although this way of thinking about evidence is not wrong, it is much too limited. Corroboration (proving the validity of a claim) is one of the functions of evidence, but not the only one.

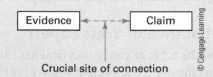

Crucial site of connection

FIGURE 6.1
Linking Evidence and Claims

It helps to remember that the word *prove* actually comes from a Latin verb meaning "to test." The noun form of prove, proof, has two meanings: (1) evidence sufficient to establish a thing as true or believable, and (2) the act of testing for truth or believability. When you operate on the basis of the first definition of proof alone, you are far more likely to seek out evidence that supports only your point of view, ignoring or dismissing other evidence that could lead to a different and possibly better idea.

The advantage to following the second definition of the word proof—in the sense of testing—is that you will be better able to negotiate among competing points of view. Doing so will predispose your readers to consider what you have to say, because you are offering them not only the thoughts a person has had, but also a person in the act of thinking. Writing well means sharing your thought process with your readers, telling them why you believe the evidence means what you say it does.

"Because I Say So": Unsubstantiated Claims

Problem: Making claims that lack supporting evidence.
Solution: Using concrete details to support and sharpen the claim.

Unsubstantiated claims occur when a writer concentrates only on conclusions, omitting the evidence that led to them. At the opposite extreme, pointless evidence results when a writer offers a mass of detail attached to an overly general claim. Both of these problems can be solved by offering readers the evidence that led to the claim and explaining how the evidence led there.

The word *unsubstantiated* means "without substance." An unsubstantiated claim is not necessarily false, it just offers none of the concrete "stuff" upon which the claim is based. When a writer makes an unsubstantiated claim, he or she has assumed that readers will believe it just because the writer put it out there. Perhaps more important, unsubstantiated claims deprive a writer of details. If you lack actual "stuff" to analyze, you tend to overstate your position and leave your readers wondering exactly what you mean.

You can see the problem of unsubstantiated assertions not only in papers but also in everyday conversation. It occurs when people get in the habit of leaping to conclusions—forming impressions so quickly and automatically that they have difficulty even recalling what triggered a particular response. Ask such people why they thought a new acquaintance is pretentious, and they will rephrase the generalization rather than offer the evidence that led to it: the person is pretentious because he puts on airs.

Simply rephrasing your generalizations rather than offering evidence starves your thinking; it also shuts out readers. If, for example, you defend your judgment that a person is pretentious by saying that he puts on airs, you have ruled on the matter and dismissed it. (You have also committed a logical flaw known as a circular argument; because "pretentious" and "putting on airs" mean virtually the same thing, using one in support of the other is arguing in a circle.)

If, by contrast, you include the grounds upon which your judgment is based—that he uses words without regard to whether his listeners will understand or that he always wears a bow tie—you have at least given readers a glimpse of your evaluative criteria. Readers are far more likely to accept your views if you give them the chance to think with you about the evidence. The alternative—offering groundless assertions—is to expect them to take your word for it.

There is, of course, an element of risk in providing the details that have informed your judgment. You leave yourself open to attack if, for example, your readers wear bow ties. But this is an essential risk to take, for otherwise, you leave your readers wondering why you think as you do, or worse, unlikely to credit your point of view.

Most importantly, taking care to substantiate your claims will make you more inclined to think openly and carefully about your judgments. And precisely because what people have taken to be common knowledge ("women can't do math," for example, or "men don't talk about their feelings") so often turns out to be wrong, you should take care to avoid unsubstantiated claims.

Distinguishing Evidence from Claims

To check your drafts for unsubstantiated assertions, you first have to know how to recognize them. It is sometimes difficult to separate facts from judgments, data from interpretations of the data. Writers who aren't practiced in this skill can believe that they are offering evidence when they are really offering only unsubstantiated claims. In your own reading and writing, pause once in a while to label the sentences of a paragraph as either evidence (E) or claims (C). What happens if we try to categorize the sentences of the following paragraph in this way?

> The owners are ruining baseball in America. Although they claim they are losing money, they are really just being greedy. Some years ago, they even fired the commissioner, Fay Vincent, because he took the players' side. Baseball is a sport, not a business, and it is a sad fact that it is being threatened by greedy businessmen.

The first and last sentences of the paragraph are claims. They draw conclusions about as yet unstated evidence that the writer will need to provide. The middle two sentences are harder to classify. If particular owners have said publicly that they are losing money, the existence of the owners' statements is a fact. But the writer moves from evidence to unsubstantiated claims when he suggests that the owners are lying about their financial situation and are doing so because of their greed. Similarly, it is a fact that Commissioner Fay Vincent was fired, but it is only an assertion that he was fired "because he took the players' side," an unsubstantiated claim. Although many of us might be inclined to accept some version of this claim as true, we should not be asked to accept the writer's opinion as self-evident truth. What is the evidence in support of the claim? What are the reasons for believing that the evidence means what the writer says it does?

The writer of the baseball paragraph, for example, offers as fact that the owners claim they are losing money. If he were to search harder, however, he would find that his statement of the owners' claim is not entirely accurate. The owners have not unanimously claimed that they are losing money; they have acknowledged that the problem has to do with poorer "small-market" teams competing against richer "large-market" teams. This more complicated version of the facts might at first be discouraging to the writer, since it reveals his original thesis ("greed") to be oversimplified. But then, as we have been saying, the function of evidence is not just to corroborate your claims, it should also help you to test and refine your ideas and to define your key terms more precisely.

Giving Evidence a Point: Making Details Speak

> **Problem:** Presenting a mass of evidence without explaining how it relates to the claims.
>
> **Solution:** Make details speak. Explain how evidence confirms and qualifies the claim.

To make your thinking visible to your readers, follow through on the implications of your evidence. You have to make the details speak, conveying to your readers why they mean what you say they mean.

The following example illustrates what happens when a writer leaves the evidence to speak for itself.

> Baseball is a sport, not a business, and it is a sad fact that it is being threatened by greedy businessmen. For example, Eli Jacobs, the previous owner of the Baltimore Orioles, sold the team to Peter Angelos for one hundred million dollars more than he had spent ten years earlier when he purchased it. Also, a new generation of baseball stadiums has been built in the last few decades—in Baltimore, Chicago, Arlington (Texas), Cleveland, San Francisco, Milwaukee, Houston, Philadelphia, Washington, and, most recently, in Miami. These parks are enormously expensive and include elaborate scoreboards and luxury boxes. The average baseball players, meanwhile, now earn more than a million dollars a year, and they all have agents to represent them. Alex Rodriguez, the third baseman for the New York Yankees, is paid more than twenty million dollars a season. Sure, he continues to set records for homers by a player at his age, but is any ballplayer worth that much money?

Unlike the previous example, which was virtually all claims, this paragraph, except for the opening claim and the closing question, is all evidence. The paragraph presents what we might call an "evidence sandwich": it encloses a series of facts between two claims. (The opening statement blames "greedy businessmen," presumably owners, and the closing statement appears to indict greedy, or at least overpaid, players.) Readers are left with two problems. First, the mismatch between the opening and concluding claims leaves it not altogether clear what the writer is saying that the evidence suggests. And second, he has not told readers why they should believe that the evidence means what he says it does. Instead, he leaves it to speak for itself.

If readers are to accept the writer's implicit claims—that the spending is too much and that it is ruining baseball—he will have to show how and why the evidence supports these conclusions. The rule that applies here is that evidence can almost always be interpreted in more than one way.

We might, for instance, formulate at least three conclusions from the evidence offered in the baseball paragraph. We might decide that the writer believes baseball will be ruined by going broke or that its spirit will be ruined by becoming too commercial. Worst of all, we might disagree with his claim and conclude that baseball is not really being ruined, because the evidence could be read as signs of health rather than decay. The profitable resale of the Orioles, the expensive new ballparks (which, the writer neglects to mention, have drawn record crowds), and the skyrocketing salaries all could testify to the growing popularity, rather than the decline, of the sport.

How to Make Details Speak: A Brief Example The best way to begin making the details speak is to take the time to look at them, asking questions about what they imply.

1. Say explicitly what you take the details to mean.

2. State exactly how the evidence supports your claims.

3. Consider how the evidence complicates (qualifies) your claims.

The writer of the baseball paragraph leaves some of his claims and virtually all of his reasoning about the evidence implicit. What, for example, bothers him about the special luxury seating areas? Attempting to uncover his assumptions, we might speculate that he intends it to demonstrate how economic interests are taking baseball away from its traditional fans because these new seats cost more than the average person can afford. This interpretation could be used to support the writer's governing claim, but he would need to spell out the connection, to reason back to his own premises. He might say, for example, that baseball's time-honored role as the all-American sport—democratic and grass-roots—is being displaced by the tendency of baseball as a business to attract higher box office receipts and wealthier fans.

The writer could then make explicit what his whole paragraph implies: that baseball's image as a popular pastime in which all Americans can participate is being tarnished by players and owners alike, whose primary concerns appear to be making money. In making his evidence speak in this way, the writer would be practicing step 3 above—using the evidence to complicate and refine his ideas. He would discover which specific aspect of baseball he thinks is being ruined, clarifying that the "greedy businessmen" to whom he refers include both owners and players.

Let's emphasize the final lesson gleaned from this example. When you focus on tightening the links between evidence and claim, the result is almost always a "smaller" claim than the one you set out to prove. This is what evidence characteristically does to a claim: it shrinks and restricts its scope. This process is known as qualifying a claim.

Sometimes it is hard to give up on the large, general assertions that were your first responses to your subject. But your sacrifices in scope are exchanged for greater accuracy and validity. The sweeping claims you lose ("Greedy businessmen are ruining baseball") give way to less resounding— but also more informed, more incisive, and less judgmental—ideas ("Market pressures may not bring the end of baseball, but they are certainly changing the image and nature of the game").

More than Just "the Facts": What Counts as Evidence?

Thus far this chapter has concentrated on how to use evidence after you've assembled it. In many cases, though, a writer has to consider a more basic and often hidden question before collecting data: what counts as evidence?

This question raises two related concerns:

Relevance: in what ways does the evidence bear on the claim or problem that you are addressing? Do the facts really apply in this particular case, and if so, how?

Framing assumptions: in what ways is the evidence colored by the point of view that designated it as evidence? At what point does this coloring undercut the authority or reliability of the evidence?

To raise the issue of framing assumptions is not to imply that all evidence is merely subjective, somebody's impressionistic opinion. We are implying, however, that even the most apparently neutral evidence is the product of some way of seeing that qualifies the evidence as evidence in the first place. In some cases, this way of seeing is embedded in the established procedure of particular disciplines. In the natural sciences, for example, the actual data that go into the results section of a lab report or formal paper are the product of a highly controlled experimental procedure. As its name suggests, the section presents the results of seeing in a particular way.

The same kind of control is present in various quantitative operations in the social sciences, in which the evidence is usually framed in the language of statistics. And in somewhat less systematic—but nonetheless similar—ways, evidence in the humanities and in some projects in the social sciences is conditioned by methodological assumptions. A literature student cannot assume, for example, that a particular fate befalls a character in a story because of events in the author's life (it is a given of literary study that biography may inform, but does not explain, a work of art). Evidence is never just some free-floating, absolutely reliable, objective entity for the casual observer to sample at random. It is always a product of certain starting assumptions and procedures that readers must take into account.

Now that you understand how to better link evidence with claims, let's think about how to organize those connections in your writing. *Writing Analytically* uses the terms 1 on 10 and 10 on 1 to describe two contrasting strategies for approaching the relationship between evidence and claims. Many less-experienced writers rely heavily on 1 on 10: taking one major claim and applying it to a number of examples. For example, a persuasive paper might claim that "children have been harmed by unhealthy school lunches" and then go on to provide numerous news reports illustrating the claim. In graphical form, this process might look something like this:

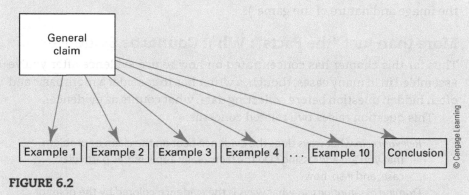

FIGURE 6.2

Doing 1 on 10: 1 Claim, 10 Pieces of Evidence (in which 10 stands arbitrarily for any number of examples)

As *Writing Analytically* explains, however, this method has its drawbacks.

The single biggest potential problem in 1 on 10 papers is that the form lends itself so easily to superficial thinking. This is true in part because when the time comes to compose a formal paper, it is very common for writers to panic, and abandon the wealth of data and ideas they have accumulated in the exploratory writing stage, telling themselves, "Now I better have my one idea and be able to prove to everybody that I'm right." Out goes careful attention to detail. Out goes any evidence that doesn't fit. Instead of analysis, they substitute the kind of paper we call a *demonstration*. That is, they cite evidence to prove that a generalization is generally true. The problem with the demonstration lies with its too limited notions of what a thesis and evidence can do in a piece of analytical thinking.

The 1 on 10 demonstration, as opposed to a more productive deductive analysis, results from a mistaken assumption about the function of evidence: that it exists only to demonstrate the validity of (corroborate) a claim. Beyond corroborating claims, evidence should serve to test and develop them. A writer who makes a single and usually very general claim ("History repeats itself," "Exercise is good for you," and so forth) and then proceeds to affix it to ten examples is likely to produce a list, not a piece of developed thinking.

1 on 10, of course, is not the only way to organize your thinking. Think back to the school lunches example: what if the paper started by explaining a single instance of an unhealthy lunch, and then explored why and how it came be: budget cuts to the school district, marketing by fast food companies, popularity of certain food items among students, etc. This is an example of doing 10 on 1: looking at one central example from many angles in order to draw out a more complex, nuanced analysis. Based on your analysis, you may then be able to apply your conclusions to other examples to gain a broader understanding.

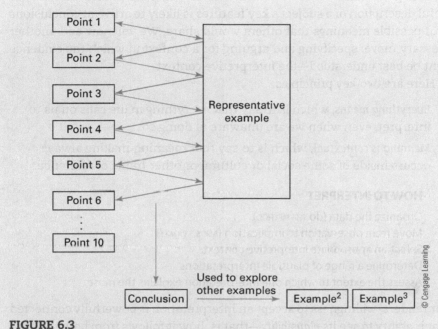

FIGURE 6.3
Doing 10 on 1. The pattern of 10 on 1 (in which "10" stands arbitrarily for any number of points) successively develops a series of points about a single representative example. Its analysis of evidence is in depth

Writing Analytically describes the benefits of 10 on 1 this way:

The practice of DOING 10 ON 1 remedies the major problem writers have when they do 1 on 10: simply attaching a host of examples to an obvious and overly general claim, with little or no analysis. DOING 10 ON 1 requires writers to explore the evidence, not just generalize about it.

You can use 10 on 1 to accomplish various ends: (1) to locate the range of possible meanings your evidence suggests, (2) to make you less inclined to cling to your first claim, (3) to open the way for you to discover the complexity of your subject, and (4) to slow down the rush to generalization and thus help to ensure that when you arrive at a working thesis, it will be more specific and better able to account for your evidence.

Making Interpretations Plausible

While organizing your evidence and the claims you make about them, you may have realized a truth that sometimes unsettles beginning writers: all of this is open to interpretation. The following section of *Writing Analytically* will help you to understand what may make one interpretation better, more interesting, or more useful than another.

The book has so far offered two kinds of prompts for making interpretive leaps: ranking (what is most important, or interesting, or revealing and why?) and asking "So What?" We've also demonstrated that the writer who can offer careful description of a subject's key features is likely to arrive at conclusions about possible meanings that others would share. We will now add another necessary move: specifying and arguing for a context in which the evidence might be best understood—the **interpretive context.**

Here are two key principles:

- *Everything means,* which is to say that everything in life calls on us to interpret, even when we are unaware of doing so.

- *Meaning is contextual,* which is to say that meaning-making always occurs inside of some social or cultural or other frame of reference.

HOW TO INTERPRET

Organize the data (do THE METHOD)
Move from observation to implication (ASK SO WHAT?)
Select an appropriate interpretive context
Determine a range of plausible interpretations
Assess the extent to which one interpretation explains the most

Your readers' willingness to accept an interpretation is powerfully connected to their ability to see its *plausibility*—that is, how it follows from both the supporting details that you have selected and the language you have used in characterizing those details. *An interpretive conclusion is not a fact, but a theory.* Interpretive conclusions stand or fall not so much on whether they can be proved right or wrong, but on whether they are demonstrably plausible. Often the best that you can hope for with interpretive conclusions is not that others will say, "Yes, that is obviously right," but "Yes, I can see where it might be possible and reasonable to think as you do."

Meanings must be reasoned from sufficient evidence if they are to be judged plausible. Meanings can always be refuted by people who find fault with your reasoning or can cite conflicting evidence. Let's refer back briefly to a hypothetical interpretation raised in Chapter 4's discussion of *Whistler's Mother*: that the woman in the painting who is clad in black is mourning the death of a loved one, perhaps a person who lived in the house represented in the painting on the wall. It is true that black clothes often indicate mourning. This is a culturally accepted sign. But with only the black dress and perhaps the sad facial expression (if it is sad) to go on, this "mourning theory" gets sidetracked from what is actually in the painting and moves into storytelling. Insufficient evidence would make this theory implausible.

Now, what if another person asserted that Whistler's mother is an alien astronaut, for example, her long black dress concealing a third leg? Obviously, this interpretation would not win wide support, and for a reason that points up another of the primary limits on the meaning-making process: meanings, to have value outside one's own private realm of experience, have to make sense to other people. This is to say that the relative value of interpretive meanings is to some extent socially (culturally) determined. The assertion that Whistler's mother is an alien astronaut is unlikely to be deemed acceptable by enough people to give it currency.

Although people are free to say that things mean whatever they want them to mean, saying doesn't make it so. The mourning theory has more evidence than the alien astronaut theory, but it still relies too heavily on what is not there, on a narrative for which there is insufficient evidence in the painting itself.

In experimental science, it is especially important that a writer/researcher be able to locate his or her work in the context of other scientists who have achieved similar results. Isolated results and interpretations, those that are not corroborated by others' research, have much less credibility. In this respect, the making of meaning is collaborative and communal. The collaborative nature of scientific and scholarly work is one of the reasons that writing about reading is so important in college-level writing. In order to interpret evidence in a way that others will find plausible, you first have to have some idea of what others in the field are talking about.

Context and the Making of Meaning

Most interpretations that people are willing to accept as plausible occur inside some social or cultural context. They are valid according to a given point of view—what the social commentator Stanley Fish has called an "interpretive community." We'll now try to answer questions posed at the chapter's opening—what makes some interpretations better than others? And what makes interpretations more than a matter of personal opinion?

Regardless of how the context is arrived at, an important part of getting an interpretation accepted as plausible is to argue for the appropriateness of the interpretive context you use, not just the interpretation it takes you to. *An interpretive context is a lens.* Depending on the context you choose—preferably a context suggested by the evidence itself—you will see different things.

Different interpretations will account better for some details than others—which is why it enriches our view of the world to try on different interpretations. Ultimately, you will have to decide which possible interpretation, as seen through which plausible interpretive context, best accounts for what you think is most important and interesting to notice about your subject.

Consider, for example, a reading of *Whistler's Mother* that a person might produce if he or she began with noticing the actual title, *Arrangement in Grey and Black: The Artist's Mother*. From this starting point, a person might focus exclusively on the disposition of color and arrive at an interpretation that the painting is about painting (which might then explain why there is also a painting on the wall).

The figure of the mother then would have meaning only insofar as it contained the two colors mentioned in the painting's title, black and gray, and the painting's representational content (the aspects of life that it shows us) would be assigned less importance. This is a promising and plausible idea for an interpretation. It makes use of different details from previous interpretations that we've suggested, but it would also address some of the details already targeted (the dress, the curtain) from an entirely different context.

To generalize: two equally plausible interpretations can be made of the same thing. It is not the case that our first reading (in Chapter 4), focusing on the profile view of the mother and suggesting the painting's concern with mysterious separateness, is right, whereas the painting-about-painting (or aesthetic) view, building from the clue in the title, is wrong. They operate within different contexts.

Specifying an Interpretive Context: A Brief Example

Notice how in the following analysis the student writer's interpretation relies on his choice of a particular interpretive context, post-World War II Japan. Had he selected another context, he might have arrived at different conclusions about the same details. Notice also how the writer perceives a pattern in the details and queries his own observations ("So what?") to arrive at an interpretation.

> The series entitled "Kamaitachi" is a journal of the photographer Hosoe's desolate childhood and wartime evacuation in the Tokyo countryside. He returns years later to the areas where he grew up, a stranger to his native land, perhaps likening himself to the legendary Kamaitachi, an invisible sickle-toothed weasel, intertwined with the soil and its unrealized fertility. "Kamaitachi #8" (1956), a platinum palladium print, stands alone to best capture Hosoe's alienation from and troubled expectation of the future of Japan. [Here the writer chooses the photographer's life as his interpretive context.]

> The image is that of a tall fence of stark horizontal and vertical rough wood lashed together, looming above the barren rice fields. Straddling the fence, half-crouched and half-clinging, is a solitary male figure, gazing in profile to the horizon. Oblivious to the sky above of dark and churning thunderclouds, the figure instead focuses his attentions and concentrations elsewhere. [The writer selects and describes significant detail.]

> It is exactly this *elsewhere* that makes the image successful, for in studying the man we are to turn our attention in the direction of the figure's gaze and away from the photograph itself. He hangs curiously between heaven and earth, suspended on a makeshift man-made structure, in a purgatorial limbo awaiting the future. He waits with anticipation—perhaps dread?—for a time that has not yet come; he is directed

away from the present, and it is this sensitivity to time which sets this print apart from the others in the series. One could argue that in effect this man, clothed in common garb, has become Japan itself, indicative of the post-war uncertainty of a country once-dominant and now destroyed. What will the future (dark storm clouds) hold for this newly humbled nation? [Here the writer notices a pattern of in-between-ness and locates it in an historical context in order to make his interpretive leap.]

Remember that regardless of the subject you select for your analysis, you should directly address not just "What does this say?" but also, as this writer has done, "What are we invited to make of it, and in what context?"

Intention as an Interpretive Context

An interpretive context that frequently creates problems in analysis is intention. People relying on authorial intention as their interpretive context typically assert that the author—not the work itself—is the ultimate and correct source of interpretations.

Look at the drawing titled *The Dancers* in Figure 6.4. What follows is the artist's statement about how the drawing came about and what it came to mean to her.

> This piece was created completely unintentionally. I poured some ink onto paper and blew on it through a straw. The ink took the form of what looked like little people in movement. I recopied the figures I liked, touched up the rough edges, and ended with this gathering of fairy-like creatures. I love how in art something abstract can so suddenly become recognizable.

In this case, interestingly, the artist initially had no intentions beyond experimenting with materials. As the work evolved, she began to arrive at her own interpretation of what the drawing might suggest. Most viewers would probably find the artist's interpretation plausible, but this is not to say that the artist must have the last word and that it is somehow an infraction for others to produce alternative interpretations.

© The Dancers, by Sarah Kersh. Pen and ink drawing. 6" × 13.75". Used by Permission of Sarah Kersh.

FIGURE 6.4
The Dancers by Sarah Kersh

Suppose the artist had stopped with her first two sentences. Even this explicit statement of her lack of intention would not prohibit people from interpreting the drawing in some of the ways that she later goes on to suggest. The artist's initial absence of a plan doesn't require viewers to interpret *The Dancers* as only ink on paper.

Whenever an intention is ascribed to a person or an act or a product, this intention contributes significantly to meaning; but the intention, whatever its source, does not outrank or exclude other interpretations. It is simply another context for understanding.

Here is another example. In the early 1960s, a popular domestic sitcom entitled *Leave It to Beaver* portrayed the mother, June Cleaver, usually impeccably dressed in heels, dress, and pearls, doing little other than dusting the mantelpiece and making tuna fish sandwiches for her sons. Is the show then intentionally implying that the proper role for women is that of domestic helper? Well, in the context of post-women's movement thinking, the show's representation of Mrs. Cleaver might plausibly be read this way, but not as a matter of intention. To conclude that *Leave It to Beaver* promoted a particular stereotype about women does not mean that the writers got together every week and thought out ways to do so.

It is interesting and useful to try to determine from something you are analyzing what its makers might have intended. But, by and large, you are best off concentrating on what the thing itself communicates as opposed to what someone might have wanted it to communicate.

What Is and Isn't "Meant" to Be Analyzed

What about analyzing things that were not intended to "mean" anything, like entertainment films and everyday things like blue jeans and shopping malls? Some people believe that it is wrong to bring out unintended implications. Let's take another example: Barbie dolls. These are just toys intended for young girls, people might say. Clearly, the intention of Mattel, the makers of Barbie, is to make money by entertaining children. Does that mean Barbie must remain outside of interpretive scrutiny for such things as her built-in earrings and high-heeled feet? What the makers of a particular product or idea intend is only a part of what that product or idea communicates.

The urge to cordon off certain subjects from analysis on the grounds that they weren't meant to be analyzed unnecessarily excludes a wealth of information—and meaning—from your range of vision. It is right to be careful about the interpretive contexts we bring to our experience. It is less right—less useful—to confine our choice of context in a too literal-minded way to a single category. To some people, baseball is only a game and clothing is only there to protect us from the elements.

What such people don't want to admit is that things communicate meaning to others whether we wish them to or not, which is to say that the meanings of most things are socially determined. What, for example, does the choice of wearing a baseball cap to a staff meeting or to a class "say"? Note, by the way, that a communicative gesture such as the wearing of a hat need not be premeditated to communicate something to other people. The hat is still "there" and available to be "read" by others as a sign of certain attitudes and a culturally defined sense of identity—with or without intention.

Baseball caps, for example, carry different associations from berets or wool caps because they come from different social contexts. Baseball caps convey a set of attitudes associated with the piece of American culture they come from. They suggest, for example, popular rather than high culture, casual rather than formal, young—perhaps defiantly so, especially if worn backward—rather than old, and so on.

We can, of course, protest that the "real" reason for turning our baseball cap backward is to allow more light in, making it easier to see than when the bill of the cap shields our faces. This practical rationale makes sense, but it does not explain away the social statement that the hat and a particular way of wearing it might make, whether or not this statement is intentional. Because meaning is, to a significant extent, socially determined, we can't entirely control what our clothing, our manners, our language, or even our way of walking communicates to others.

The social contexts that make gestures like our choice of hats carry particular meanings are always shifting, but some such context is always present. As we asserted at the beginning of this chapter, everything means, and meaning is always contextual.

Avoiding the Extremes: Neither "Fortune Cookie" nor "Anything Goes"

Two of the most common missteps in producing an interpretation are the desire for a single, right answer and, at the opposite extreme, the conviction that all explanations are equally acceptable. The first of these we call the Fortune Cookie School of Interpretation, and the latter we label the Anything Goes School.

The Fortune Cookie School of Interpretation

Proponents of the Fortune Cookie School believe that if a person can only "crack" the thing correctly—the subject, the problem—it will yield an extractable and self-contained "message." There are several problems with this conception of the interpretive process.

First, the assumption that things have single hidden meanings interferes with open-minded and dispassionate observation. Adherents of the Fortune Cookie School look solely for clues pointing to *the* hidden message and, having found these clues, discard the rest, like the cookie in a Chinese restaurant once the fortune has been extracted. The fortune cookie approach forecloses on the possibility of multiple plausible meanings, each within its own context.

When you assume that there is only one right answer, you are also assuming that there is only one proper context for understanding and, by extension, that anybody who happens to select a different starting point or context and who thus arrives at a different answer is necessarily wrong.

Most of the time, practitioners of the fortune cookie approach aren't even aware that they are assuming the correctness of a single context, because they don't realize a fundamental truth about interpretations: they are always limited by contexts. In other words, we are suggesting that claims to universal truths are problematic. Things don't just mean in some simple and clear way for all people in all situations; they always mean within a network of beliefs, from a particular point of view. The person who claims to have access to some universal truth, beyond context and point of view, is either naïve (unaware) or, worse, a bully—insisting that his or her view of the world is obviously correct and must be accepted by everyone.

The "Anything Goes" School of Interpretation

At the opposite extreme from the Fortune Cookie School lies the completely relativist Anything Goes School. The problem with the anything goes approach is that it tends to assume that *all* interpretations are equally viable, and that meanings are simply a matter of individual choice, regardless of evidence or plausibility. Put another way, it overextends the creative aspect of interpretation to absurdity, arriving at the position that you can see in a subject whatever you want to see. But such unqualified relativism is not logical. It is simply not the case that meaning is entirely up to the individual; some readings are clearly better than others. The better interpretations have more evidence and rational explanation of how the evidence supports the interpretive claims—qualities that make these meanings more public and negotiable.

Implications Versus Hidden Meanings

While some people search for a single right answer and dismiss the rest, others dismiss the interpretive project altogether. Those who adopt this latter stance are excessively literal minded; they see any venture into interpretation as a benighted quest to impose "hidden meanings" on the reader.

The phrase itself, "hidden meaning," carries implications. It suggests that meanings exist in places other than the literal words on the page: they are to be found either "under" or "between" the lines of text.

Another phrase with which they disparage the interpretive process is "reading between the lines," suggesting that we have to look for meanings elsewhere than in the lines of text themselves. At its most skeptical, the phrase "reading between the lines" means that an interpretation has come from nothing at all, from the white space between the lines, and therefore has been imposed on the material by the interpreter.

Neither of these positions is a wholly unreasonable response because each recognizes that meanings are not always overt. But responding with these phrases misrepresents the process of interpretation. To understand why, let's spell out some of the assumptions that underlie these phrases.

The charge that the meaning is hidden can imply for some people an act of conspiracy on the part of either an author, who chooses to deliberately obscure his or her meaning, or on the part of readers, who conspire to "find" things lurking below the surface that other readers don't know about and are unable to see. A further assumption is that people probably know what they mean most of the time but, for some perverse reason, are unwilling to come out and say so.

Proponents of these views of analysis are, in effect, committing themselves to the position that everything in life means what it says and says what it means. It is probably safe to assume that most writers try to write what they mean and mean what they say. That is, they try to control the range of possible interpretations that their words could give rise to, but there is always more going on in a piece of writing (as in our everyday conversation) than can easily be pinned down and controlled. It is, in fact, an inherent property of language that it always means more than, and thus other than, it says.

It is also true that a large part of human communication takes place indirectly. A good example of this is metaphor, to which we now turn.

Figurative Logic: Reasoning with Metaphors

Metaphor, it has been said, is one of the few uses of language in which it is okay to say one thing and mean another. It is, in other words, a way of communicating things via association and implication rather than direct statement. If metaphors were to be found only in poems, as some people assume, then interpreting them would be a specialized skill with narrow application. But, in fact, metaphors are deeply engrained in the language we use every day, which becomes evident as soon as we take the time to notice them.

George Lakoff, Professor of Linguistics and Cognitive Science, and English Professor, Mark Turner, among others, have demonstrated that metaphors are built into the way we think. (See Lakoff and Turner's book, *More than Cool Reason, a Field Guide to Poetic Metaphor*, University of Chicago Press, 1989.) As such, metaphors routinely constitute our assumptions about the world and our place in it. Life, for example, is a journey. To become successful you climb a ladder. Being up is a good thing. To be down is to be unhappy (or blue). These are all metaphors.

If we accept their implicit arguments in an unexamined way, metaphors can call the shots in our lives more than we should allow them to. For example, if you believe that success involves climbing a ladder, you will be more likely to feel compelled to constantly climb higher than others in an organization rather than take a chance on a horizontal move that might lead you to something more personally rewarding (and in that respect, more successful). And if you have absorbed from the culture the idea that life is a race, then you will be worried about not moving fast enough and not competing effectively with others, as opposed to collaborating or doing something different that most others are not doing, perhaps something with no obvious prize attached.

THE LOGIC OF METAPHOR

- Metaphors pervade our ways of thinking
- Metaphor is a way of thinking by analogy
- The logic of metaphors is implicit
- The implicit logic of metaphors can be made explicit by scrutinizing the language
- We can recast figurative language to see and evaluate its arguments

The fact that metaphors require interpretation—as do most uses of language—does not take away from the fact that metaphors are a way of thinking. Being able to articulate the implicit arguments embodied in metaphors—making their meanings explicit so that they can be opened to discussion with others—is an important skill to acquire.

Although figurative logic does not operate in the same way as claims-based (propositional) logic, it nevertheless produces arguments, the reasoning of which can be analyzed and evaluated *systematically*. Let's start with a definition. Metaphors and similes work by **analogy**—a type of comparison that often finds similarities between things that are otherwise unlike.

Consider the simile "My love is like a red red rose." A simile, identifiable by its use of the words "like" or "as," operates like a metaphor except that both sides of the analogy are explicitly stated. The subject of the simile, love, is called the *tenor*; the comparative term brought in to think about love, rose, is called the *vehicle*.

In metaphors, the thought connection between the vehicle (rose) and the tenor (my love) is left unstated. But for our purposes, the clearer and more explicit simile will do. It is the nature of the resemblance between the speaker's love and roses that we are invited to infer.

Here is where the process of interpreting figurative language becomes systematic. The first step in interpreting this simile is to list the characteristics of the vehicle, red roses—especially red red (very red) roses—that might be relevant in this piece of thinking by analogy. Most people find roses to be beautiful. Most people associate red with passion. In fact, science can now measure the body's response to different colors. Red produces excitement. Red can even make the pulse rate go up. Roses are also complicated flowers. Their shape is convoluted. Roses are thought of as female. Rose petals are fragile. Many roses have thorns. So, the simile is actually a piece of thinking about love and about women.

It is not a very deep piece of thinking, and probably many women would prefer that the thorn part not be made too prominent. In fact, a reader would have to decide in the context of other language in the poem whether thorniness, as a characteristic of some roses, is significant and ought to be considered. The point is that the simile does make an argument about women that could be stated overtly, analyzed and evaluated. The implication that women, like roses, might have thorns—and thus be hard to "pick," defending them from male intruders, etc.—is part of the argument.

Figure 6.5 represents the procedure for exploring the logic of metaphor.

1 **Isolate the vehicle**—the language in the metaphor that states one side of the analogy.

2 **Articulate the characteristics of the vehicle, its defining traits.**

3 **Select the characteristics of the vehicle that seem most significant in context.**

4 **Make interpretive leaps to what the metaphor communicates.** Use significant characteristics of the vehicle to prompt these leaps.

FIGURE 6.5
Interpreting Figurative Language

Notice how, in the rose example, our recasting of the original simile has made explicit the implicit meanings suggested by the figurative language. This recasting is a useful act of thinking, one that makes evident the thought process that a metaphor sets in motion.

What such recasting reveals is not only that metaphors do, in fact, make claims, but that they are remarkably efficient at doing so. A metaphor can say a lot in a little by compressing a complex amalgam of thought and feeling into a single image.

SEEMS TO BE ABOUT X, BUT COULD ALSO BE (OR IS "REALLY") ABOUT Y

When people begin to interpret something, they usually find that less obvious meanings are cloaked by more obvious ones, and so they are distracted from seeing them. In most cases, the less obvious and possibly unintended meanings are more telling and more interesting than the obvious ones they have been conditioned to see.

The person who is doing the interpreting too often stops with the first "answer" that springs to mind as he or she moves from observation to implication, often landing upon a cliché. If this first response becomes the X, then the writer is prompted to come up with other, probably less commonplace interpretations, as the Y. (See Figure 6.6.)

This prompt is based on the conviction that understandings are rarely simple and overt. Completing the formula by supplying key terms for X and Y, writers get practice in making the implicit explicit and accepting the existence

1	Start the interpretive process by filling in the blank (the X) in the statement "This subject seems to be about X." X should be an interpretive leap, not just a summary or description.
2	Pose another interpretive possibility by finishing the sentence, "but it could also be (or is really) about Y."
3	Repeat this process a number of times to provoke new interpretive leaps. In effect, you are brainstorming alternative explanations for the same phenomenon.
4	Choose what you think is the best formulation for Y and write a paragraph or more explaining your choice.

FIGURE 6.6

Doing "Seems to Be About X, But Could Also Be (Or Is "Really") About Y"

of multiple plausible meanings for something. seems to be about x is especially useful when considering the rhetoric of a piece: its complex and various ways of targeting and appealing to an audience. It's also useful for "reading against the grain"—seeking out what something is about that it probably does not know it's about.

Note: Don't be misled by our use of the word *really* in this heuristic into thinking that there should be some single, hidden, right answer. The aim is to prompt you to think recursively—to come up with a range of possible landing sites for your interpretive leap rather than just one.

Seems to Be About X . . .: An Example

A classic and highly successful television ad campaign for Nike Freestyle shoes contains sixty seconds of famous basketball players dribbling and passing and otherwise handling the ball in dexterous ways to the accompaniment of court noises and hip-hop music. The ad seems to be about X (basketball or shoes) but could also be about Y. Once you've made this assertion, a rapid-fire (brainstormed) list might follow in which you keep filling in the blanks (X and Y) with different possibilities. Alternatively, you might find that filling in the blanks (X and Y) leads to a more sustained exploration of a single point. This is your eventual goal, but doing a little brainstorming first would keep you from shutting down the interpretive process too soon.

Here is one version of a rapid-fire list, any item of which might be expanded:

> Seems to be about basketball but is "really" about dance.
> Seems to be about selling shoes but is "really" about artistry.
> Seems to be about artistry but is "really" about selling shoes.
> Seems to be about basketball but is "really" about race.
> Seems to be about basketball but is "really" about the greater acceptance of black culture in American media and society.
> Seems to be about individual expertise but is "really" about working as a group.

Here is one version of a more sustained exploration of a single SEEMS TO BE ABOUT X statement.

The Nike Freestyle commercial seems to be about basketball but is really about the greater acceptance of black culture in American media. Of course it is a shoe commercial and so aims to sell a product, but the same could be said about any commercial.

What makes the Nike commercial distinctive is its seeming embrace of African-American culture. The hip-hop sound track, for example, which coincides with the rhythmic dribbling of the basketball, places music and sport on a par, and the dexterity with which the players (actual NBA stars) move with the ball—moonwalking, doing 360s on it, balancing it on their fingers, heads, and backs—is nothing short of dance.

The intrinsic cool of the commercial suggests that Nike is targeting an audience of basketball lovers, not just African-Americans. If I am right, then it is selling blackness to white as well as black audiences. Of course, the idea that blacks are cooler than whites goes back at least as far as the early days of jazz and might be seen as its own strange form of prejudice.

CHAPTER 7

The Thesis Statement

At this point, you've had a lot of practice in analysis. You've learned how to make detailed observations; you've constructed claims based on the evidence you've gathered; you've begun to interpret your evidence with the help of secondary sources. Now, in your Analytical Research Paper, you need to bring this all together to present a coherent and well-supported interpretation of your primary source. In order to ensure that this interpretation is well supported, you will combine the analysis that you have performed and the research that you have conducted, all in conversation with your secondary sources. In order to make this interpretation clear to your reader, you will develop a strong, concise, and interesting thesis that takes into account all of the evidence you have uncovered over the course of your analysis.

Thesis or Thesis Statement?

At this stage, it is helpful to distinguish between a *thesis* and a *thesis statement*. Most English 1110 students have encountered the concept of a thesis statement in the past. However, many students view the thesis statement as a sort of summary of the essay, a sentence that says what the essay is about. It is important to realize that a thesis statement is not, in fact, a summary of the paper. Instead, it is literally a statement of the *thesis* of the paper. In order to understand this, you must understand what a thesis is.

The thesis is the central claim that the paper is making. It is the new, interesting, or significant idea that the paper is offering to its audience. As an example: while the topic of your Analytical Research Paper might be the old Apple computer advertisement that we previously discussed, the thesis of your Analytical Research Paper might be that though Apple uses the figure of Benjamin Franklin to suggest that computer buyers are revolutionary people who are ahead of their time, its emphasis on the potential consumer as male makes the company seem surprisingly conservative.

Before you can worry about the words that you will use to *state* your thesis, you need to *have* a thesis. That is: you need to come up with a single coherent central claim that you plan to make about your primary source. This claim should arise from your observations and research, and you should be able to provide a substantial amount of evidence for it.

Let's see what *Writing Analytically* has to say about the thesis—including a strategy for making your thesis stronger.

A thesis is an idea that you formulate about your subject. It should offer a theory about the meaning of evidence that would not have been immediately obvious to your readers. A weak thesis either makes no claim or makes a claim that does not need proving, such as a statement of fact or an opinion with which virtually all of your readers would agree before reading your paper (for example, "exercise is good for you").

WHAT A PRODUCTIVE THESIS DOES

Promotes thinking: leads you to arrive at ideas.

Reduces scope: separates useful evidence from the welter of details.

Provides direction: helps you decide what to talk about and what to talk about next.

WHAT A WEAK THESIS DOES

Addicts you too early to a too-large idea, so that you stop actually seeing the evidence in its real-life complexity or thinking about the idea itself.

Produces a demonstration rather than discovery of new ideas by making the same overly general point again and again about a range of evidence.

Includes too much possible data without helping you see what's most important to talk about.

Thesis-Driven Writing: Some Pros and Cons

The term "thesis" has a long history, going back to classical rhetoric wherein a thesis involved taking a position on some subject. This idea of "taking a position" is not a good fit with the methods and goals of inquiry-based writing, the orientation that most academic writing requires. In an essay entitled "Let's End Thesis Tyranny," author and professor Bruce Ballenger argues that thesis-driven writing, especially when thought of as supporting a single idea that the writer sets out to prove, is especially ill-suited to treating "complicated problems that might raise questions with multiple answers, none of them necessarily correct" (*The Chronicle of Higher Education*, July 17, 2013).

One of the most disabling misunderstandings about thesis statements is that a writer needs to have a thesis before he or she begins writing. Arriving at claims too early in the writing process blinds writers to complicating evidence (evidence that runs counter to the thesis) and so deprives them of opportunities to arrive at better ideas.

And yet, it's also true that a writer has not really "graduated" from the exploratory writing phase to the writing of an actual paper until he or she has discovered an idea around which his or her thinking can cohere. A thesis statement gives a paper a sense of purpose and provides readers with something to follow. Without a governing idea to hold onto, readers can't be expected to understand why you are telling them what you are telling them.

Here are two ways to arrive at and use thesis statements that will foster inquiry and court rather than avoid complexity:

- Focus on an area of your subject that is open to opposing viewpoints or multiple interpretations, and

- Treat the thesis at which you arrive as a hypothesis to be tested, rather than an obvious truth.

In sum, the thesis needs to be a stimulus to the exploration of ideas—not a tyrant that reduces complex matters to oversimplified formulations.

Coming Up with a Thesis: What It Means to Have an Idea

Thesis statements are the result of having an idea about your subject. Thus, it makes sense to pause and consider what it means to have an idea. You can probably best understand what it means by considering what ideas do and where they can be found. Here is a partial list:

- An idea usually starts with an observation that is puzzling, with something that you want to figure out rather than something that you think you already understand.

- An idea often accounts for some dissonance, something that seems not to fit together.

- An idea may be the discovery of a question where there seemed not to be one.

- An idea may make explicit and explore the meaning of something implicit—an unstated assumption upon which an argument rests or a logical consequence of a given position.

- An idea may connect elements of a subject and explain the significance of that connection.

As this list demonstrates, ideas are likely to arise when there is something to negotiate—when you require yourself not just to list answers, but to ask questions, make choices, and engage in reasoning about the meaning and significance of your evidence.

How to Word Thesis Statements

The wording and syntax (sentence structure) of thesis statements have shaping force in the way a paper develops. Some thesis shapes are more effective than others. Here in condensed form is the advice offered in the upcoming discussion of thesis shapes:

- A productive thesis usually contains *tension*, the balance of this against that.

- Effective thesis statements often begin with a grammatically subordinate idea that will get outweighed by a more pressing claim: "Although X appears to account for Z, Y accounts for it better."

- A less effective thesis shape is the list.

- Active verbs and specific nouns produce strong thesis statements.

Put X in Tension with Y

One of the best and most common ways of bringing the thesis into focus is by pitting one possible point of view against another. Good ideas usually take place with the aid of some kind of back pressure, by which we mean that the idea takes shape by pushing against another way of seeing things. This is not the same as setting out to overturn and completely refute one idea in favor of another. In good thesis statements both ideas have some validity, but the forward momentum of the thesis comes from playing the preferred idea off the other one.

Look at the following two thesis statements. Notice that there is tension in each, which results from the defining pressure of one idea against another potentially viable idea.

- It may not seem like it, but "Nice Pants" is as radical a campaign as the original Dockers series.

- If opponents of cosmetic surgery are too quick to dismiss those who claim great psychological benefits, proponents are far too willing to dismiss those who raise concerns. Cosmetic surgery might make individual people happier, but in the aggregate it makes life worse for everyone.

In the first thesis sentence, the primary idea is that the new advertising campaign for Dockers trousers is radical. The back pressure against which this idea takes shape is that this new campaign may not seem radical. The writer will demonstrate the truth of both of these claims, rather than overturning one and then championing the other.

The same can be said of the parts of the second thesis statement. One part of the thesis makes claims for the benefits of cosmetic surgery. The forward momentum of the thesis statement comes from the back pressure of this idea against the idea that cosmetic surgery will also make life worse for everyone. Notice that the thesis statement does not simply say, "Cosmetic surgery is bad." The writer's job will be to demonstrate that the potential harm of cosmetic surgery outweighs the benefits, but the benefits won't just be dismissed. Both ideas are to some extent true. Neither idea, in other words, is "a straw man"—the somewhat deceptive argumentative practice of setting up a dummy position solely because it is easy to knock down. A straw man does not strengthen a thesis statement because it fails to provide genuine back pressure.

Thesis Shapes: Subordination Versus Listing

The tension between ideas in a thesis statement is often reflected in the statement's grammatical structure. Thesis statements often combine two possible claims into one formulation, with the primary claim in the main clause and the qualifying or limiting or opposing claim in a subordinate clause: "Although X appears to account for Z, Y accounts for it better." You can more or less guarantee your thesis will possess the necessary tension by starting your thesis statement with the word "Although" or with the phrase "While it seems that . . ." or with the "yes, but" or "if x, nonetheless y" formulation. (See Chapter 10 on subordination.)

The advantage of this subordinate construction (and the reason that so many theses are set up this way) is that the subordinated idea helps you to define your own position by giving you something to define it against. The subordinate clause of a thesis helps you to demonstrate that there is, in fact, an issue involved—that is, more than one possible explanation for the evidence you are considering.

The order of clauses in a thesis statement often predicts the shape of the paper, guiding both the writer and the reader. A thesis that begins with a subordinate clause ("Although X . . . ") usually leads to a paper in which the first part deals with the claims for X and then moves to fuller embrace of Y.

A less effective thesis shape that can also predict the shape of a paper is the *list*. This is the shape of five-paragraph form: the writer lists three points and then devotes a paragraph to each. But the list does not specify the connections among its various components, and, as a result, the writer is less inclined to explore the relationship among ideas.

How to Revise Weak Thesis Statements: Make the Verbs Active and the Nouns Specific

Weak thesis statements can be quickly identified by their word choice and syntax (sentence structure). Take, for example, the thesis statement "There are many similarities and differences between the Carolingian and Burgundian Renaissances." This thesis relies mostly on nouns rather than verbs; the nouns announce a broad heading, but the verb doesn't do anything with or to the nouns. In grammatical terms, such thesis statements don't predicate (affirm or assert something about the subject of a proposition). Instead, they rely on anemic verbs like *is* or *are*, which function as equal signs that link general nouns with general adjectives rather than specify more complex relationships.

Replacing *is* or *are* with stronger verbs usually causes you to rank ideas in some order of importance, to assert some conceptual relation among them, and to advance some sort of claim. Thus, we could revise the weak thesis above as "The differences between the Carolingian and Burgundian Renaissances outweigh the similarities." While this reformulation remains quite general, it at least begins to direct the writer along a more particular line of argument.

In sum, the best way to remedy the problem of the overly broad thesis is to move toward specificity in word choice, in sentence structure, and in idea. If you find yourself writing "The economic situation is bad," consider revising it to "The tax policies of the current administration threaten to reduce the tax burden on the middle class by sacrificing education and health care programs for everyone."

Here's the problem/solution in schematic form:

Broad Noun	+ Weak Verb	+ Vague, Evaluative Modifier
The economic situation	is	bad

Specific Noun	+ Active Verb	+ Specific Modifier
(The) tax policies (of the current administration)	threaten to reduce (the tax burden on the middle class)	by sacrificing education and health care programs for everyone

By eliminating the weak thesis formula—broad noun plus is plus vague evaluative adjective—a writer is compelled to qualify, or define carefully, each of the terms in the original proposition, arriving at a more particular and conceptually rich assertion.

Is It Okay to Phrase a Thesis as a Question?

The answer is yes and no. Phrasing a thesis as a question makes it more difficult for both the writer and the reader to be sure of the direction the paper will take, because a question doesn't make an overt claim. Questions, however, can clearly imply claims. And many writers, especially in the early, exploratory stages of drafting, will begin with a question.

As a general rule, use thesis questions cautiously, particularly in final drafts. While a thesis question often functions well to spark your thinking, it can allow you to evade the responsibility of making some kind of claim. Especially in the drafting stage, a question posed overtly can provide focus, but only if you then answer it with what could become a first statement of thesis—a working thesis.

Making a Thesis Evolve

Another common misunderstanding about the thesis is that it must appear throughout the paper in essentially the same form—fixed and unchanging. In fact, it is only a weakly developed thesis that, like an inert (unreactive) material, neither makes anything happen nor undergoes any change itself. Think of the thesis as an agent of change. The thesis itself changes in an inductive essay. In a deductive essay, the thesis changes the way readers understand the range and implications of that claim.

Developing a Thesis Is More than Repeating an Idea

Weak thesis statements (poorly formulated and inadequately developed) are most easily detected by their repetitiveness and predictability. The writer says the same thing again and again, drawing the same overgeneralized conclusion from each piece of evidence ("and so, once again we see that . . .").

Weak thesis statements tend to produce demonstrations. Demonstrations point at something—"See?"—and then they're done with it. Demonstrations are not really interested in seeing into things—only at looking at them from a distance to confirm a point. The staple of the demonstration is five-paragraph form, which many writers learned in high school. The form predisposes the writer to begin with a big claim, such as "Environmentalism prevents economic growth," and then offer a paragraph on each of three examples (say, statutes that protect endangered wildlife, inhibit drilling for oil, and levy excessive fines on violators). Then the big claim simply gets repeated again in the conclusion.

At the least, such a thesis is inaccurate. It's too easy to find exceptions to the claim and also to question what its key words actually mean. Mightn't environmentalism also promote economic growth by, say, promoting tourism? And is the meaning of economic growth self-evident? Couldn't a short-term economic boon be a long-term disaster, as might be the case for oil exploration in the polar regions?

In contrast, in nearly all good writing the thesis gains in complexity as well as precision and accuracy as the paper progresses. Developing a thesis, in other words, means making the paper's thinking evolve, pruning and shaping it in response to evidence.

In cases where the thesis itself cannot evolve, as, for example, in the report format of the natural and social sciences where the initial hypothesis must be either confirmed or denied, there is still movement (conceptual development) between the beginning of the paper and the end, rather than repeated assertion of one idea.

The Thesis as Lens: The Reciprocal Relationship Between Thesis and Evidence

One function of the thesis is to provide the connective tissue, so to speak, that holds together a paper's three main parts—beginning, middle, and end. Periodic reminders of your paper's thesis, its central unifying idea, are essential for keeping both you and your readers on track. But there is a big difference between developing and just repeating an idea.

It is in establishing this key difference between development and repetition that the analogy of thesis as connective tissue breaks down. A better way of envisioning how a thesis operates is to think of it as a camera lens. The advantage of this analogy is that it more accurately describes the relationship between the thesis and the subject it seeks to explain: while the lens affects how we see the subject (what evidence we select, what questions we ask about that evidence), the subject we are looking at affects how we adjust the lens.

The relationship between thesis and subject is, in other words, reciprocal. In good analytical writing, especially in the earlier, investigatory stages of writing and thinking, the thesis not only directs the writer's way of looking at evidence, the analysis of evidence should also direct and redirect (bring about revision of) the thesis. Even in a final draft, writers are usually adjusting—fine-tuning—their governing idea in response to their analysis of evidence.

The enemy of good analytical writing is the fuzzy lens—imprecisely worded thesis statements. Very broad thesis statements, those that are made up of imprecise (fuzzy) terms, make bad camera lenses. They blur everything together, muddying important distinctions. If your lens is insufficiently sharp, you are not likely to see much in your evidence. If you say, for example, that education is costly, you will at least have some sense of direction, a means of moving forward in your paper, but the imprecise terms "education" and "costly" don't provide you with a focus clear enough to distinguish significant detail in your evidence. Without significant detail for you to analyze, you can't develop your thesis, either by showing readers what the thesis is good for (what it allows us to understand and explain) or by refining and clarifying its terms.

Evolving a Thesis in an Exploratory Draft: The Example of *Las Meninas*

Because the writing process is a way not just of recording but of discovering ideas, writers, especially in the early stages of drafting, often set out with one idea or direction in mind and then, in the process of writing, happen upon another, potentially better idea that only begins to emerge in the draft. Once you've recognized them, these emerging thoughts may lead to your evolving a markedly different thesis, or they may provide you with the means of extending your paper's original thesis well beyond the point you'd settled for initially.

Writers undertake this kind of conceptual revision—locating and defining the thesis—in different ways. Some writers rely on repeatedly revising while they work their way through a first draft (which, when finished, will be close to a final draft). Others move through the first draft without much revision and then comprehensively rethink and restructure it (sometimes two, three, or more times). Whatever mode of revision works best for you, the thinking processes we demonstrate here are central. They are the common denominators of the various stages of the drafting process.

Our means of demonstrating how writers use exploratory writing to locate and develop a workable thesis is to take you through the steps a student writer would follow in revising her initial draft on a painting, *Las Meninas* (Spanish for "the ladies in waiting") by the seventeenth-century painter, Diego Velázquez. We are using a paper on a painting because all of the writer's data (the details of the painting) are on one page, allowing you to think with the writer as she develops her ideas.

As you read the draft, watch how the writer goes about developing the claim made at the end of her first paragraph—that, despite its complexity, the painting clearly reveals at least some of the painter's intentions (referred to elsewhere in the paper as what the painting is saying, what it suggests, or what the painter wants). We have underlined each appearance of potential thesis statements in the text of the paper. Using square brackets at the ends of paragraphs, we have described the writer's methods for arriving at ideas: NOTICE AND FOCUS, THE METHOD, ASKING "SO WHAT?," and 10 ON 1 (see Chapters 4 and 6).

There are a number of good things about this student paper when considered as an exploratory draft. Studying it will help you train yourself to turn a more discriminating eye on your own works in progress, especially in that all-important early stage in which you are writing in order to discover ideas.

Velázquez's Intentions in *Las Meninas*

[1] Velázquez has been noted as being one of the best Spanish artists of all time. It seems that as Velázquez got older, his paintings became better. Toward the end of his life, he painted his masterpiece, *Las Meninas*. Out of all his works, *Las Meninas* is the only known self-portrait of Velázquez. There is much to be said about *Las Meninas*. The painting is very complex, but some of the intentions that Velázquez had in painting *Las Meninas* are very clear. **[The writer opens with background information and a broad working thesis (underlined).]**

[2] First, we must look at the painting as a whole. The question that must be answered is: who is in the painting? The people are all members of the Royal Court of the Spanish monarch Philip IV. In the center is the king's daughter, who eventually became Empress of Spain. Around her are her *meninas* or ladies-in-waiting. These *meninas* are all daughters of influential men. To the right of the *meninas* is a dwarf who is a servant, and the family dog who looks fierce but is easily tamed by the foot of a child. The more unique people in the painting are Velázquez, himself, who stands to the left in front of a large canvas; the king and queen, whose faces are captured in the obscure mirror; the man in the doorway; and the nun and man behind the *meninas*. To analyze this painting further, the relationship between characters must be understood. **[The writer describes the evidence and arrives at an operating assumption—focusing on the relationship among characters.]**

[3] Where is this scene occurring? Most likely it is in the palace. But why is there no visible furniture? Is it because Velázquez didn't want the viewers to become distracted from his true intentions? I believe it is to show that this is not just a painting of an actual event. This is an event out of his imagination. **[The writer begins pushing observations to tentative conclusions by ASKING SO WHAT?]**

[4] Now, let us become better acquainted with the characters. The child in the center is the most visible. All the light is shining on her. Maybe Velázquez is suggesting that she is the next light for Spain and that even God has approved her by shining all the available light on her. Back in those days there was a belief in the divine right of kings, so this just might be what Velázquez is saying. **[The writer starts ranking evidence for importance and continues to ask, SO WHAT?; she arrives at a possible interpretation of the painter's intention.]**

FIGURE 7.1
Las Meninas by Diego Velázquez, 1656. Approximately 10'5" × 9'. Museo del Prado, Madrid.

[5] The next people of interest are the ones behind the *meninas*. The woman in the habit might be a nun and the man a priest.

[6] The king and queen are the next group of interesting people. They are in the mirror, which is to suggest they are present, but they are not as visible as they might be. Velázquez suggests that they are not always at the center where everyone would expect them to be. **[The writer continues using NOTICE AND FOCUS plus asking SO WHAT?; in addition to looking for pattern in the painting's details, the writer has begun to notice evidence—the minimal presence of the king and queen in the painting—that could complicate her initial interpretation about the divine right of kings.]**

[7] The last person and the most interesting is Velázquez. He dominates the painting along with the little girl. He takes up the whole left side along with his gigantic easel. But what is he painting? As I previously said, he might be

painting the king and queen. But I also think he could be pretending to paint us, the viewers. The easel really gives this portrait an air of mystery because Velázquez knows that we, the viewers, want to know what he is painting. **[The writer starts doing 10 ON 1 with her selection of what she has selected as the most significant detail—the size and prominence of the painter.]**

[8] The appearance of Velázquez is also interesting. His eyes are focused outward here. They are not focused on what is going on around him. It is a steady stare. Also interesting is his confident stance. He was confident enough to place himself in the painting of the royal court. <u>I think that Velázquez wants the king to give him the recognition he deserves by including him in the "family."</u> And the symbol on his vest is the symbol given to a painter by the king to <u>show that his status and brilliance have been appreciated by the monarch</u>. It is unknown how it got there. It is unlikely that Velázquez put it there himself. That would be too outright, and Velázquez was the type to give his messages subtly. Some say that after Velázquez's death, King Philip IV himself painted it to finally <u>give Velázquez the credit he deserved for being a loyal friend and servant</u>. **[The writer continues DOING 10 ON 1 and asking SO WHAT? about the painter's appearance; this takes her to three tentative theses (underlined above).]**

[9] I believe that Velázquez was very ingenious by putting his thoughts and feelings into a painting. He didn't want to offend the king, who had done so much for him. It paid off for Velázquez because he did finally get what he wanted, even if it was after he died. **[The writer concludes and is now ready to redraft to tighten links between evidence and claims, formulate a better working thesis, and make this thesis evolve.]**

From Details to Ideas: Arriving at a Working Thesis in an Exploratory Draft

An exploratory draft uses writing as a means of arriving at a working thesis that the next draft can more fully evolve. Most writers find that their best ideas emerge near the end of the exploratory draft, which is the case in this student draft (see the three claims underlined in paragraph 8).

The *Las Meninas* paper is a good exploratory draft. The writer has begun to interpret details and draw plausible conclusions from what she sees, rather than just describing the scene depicted on the canvas or responding loosely to it with her unanalyzed impressions. The move from description to analysis and interpretation begins when you select certain details in your evidence as more important than others and explain what they seem to you to suggest. The writer has done both of these things, and so has gotten to the point where she can begin methodically evolving her initial ideas into a perceptive analysis.

What is especially good about the draft is that it reveals the writer's willingness to push on from her first idea (reading the painting as an endorsement of the divine right of kings, expressed by the light shining on the princess) by seeking out complicating evidence. The process of revising for ideas begins in earnest when you start checking to make sure that the thesis you have formulated accounts for as much of the available evidence as possible and does not avoid evidence that might complicate or contradict it.

The writer's first idea (about divine right), for example, does not account for enough of the evidence and is undermined by evidence that clearly doesn't fit, such as the small size and decentering of the king and queen, and the large size and foregrounding of the painter himself. Rather than ignoring these troublesome details, the writer instead zooms in on them. She focuses on the painter's representation of himself and of his employers, the king and queen, as the 1 for DOING 10 ON 1 (making a number of observations about a single representative piece of evidence and analyzing it in depth).

Six Steps for Finding and Evolving a Thesis in an Exploratory Draft
Getting the thesis to respond more fully to evidence, either by formulating a mostly new thesis and beginning again, or by modifying the existing thesis, is the primary activity of conceptual revision (as opposed to correcting and editing). Your aim here is not to go round and round forever, but to go back and forth between thesis and evidence, evidence and thesis, allowing each, in turn, to adjust how you see the other, until you find the best possible fit between the two. As we say in the section of this chapter on the thesis as camera lens, the thesis not only directs a writer's way of looking at evidence; the analysis of evidence should also direct and redirect—bring about revision of—the thesis.

What follows is a six-step guide for formulating and reformulating (evolving) a thesis. As an overarching guideline, allow your thesis to run up against potentially conflicting evidence ("but what about this?") in order to build upon and revise your initial idea, extending the range of evidence it can accurately account for by clarifying and qualifying its key terms.

Here is a list of the six steps:

1. Formulate a working thesis or, in revision, locate multiple and possibly competing thesis statements in your draft.

2. Explain how the details you have focused on in the evidence lead to your working thesis.

3. Locate evidence that is not adequately accounted for by the working thesis and pursue the implications of that evidence by repeatedly ASKING "SO WHAT?" Explain how and why these pieces of evidence complicate the working thesis.

4. Use your analysis of the complicating evidence to reformulate the thesis. Share with readers your reasons for moving from your initial claim to this reformulation.

5. Test the adequacy of the evolved thesis by repeating steps two, three, and four until you are satisfied that the thesis statement accounts for your evidence as fully and accurately as possible. The best test of a thesis is to see how much of the relevant evidence it can reasonably account for.

6. Rewrite the draft into a more coherent and fuller analysis of evidence, while retaining for readers the "thesis trail"—the various steps that you went through along the way to formulating the thesis you ultimately chose.

Step 1: Formulate a working thesis or, in revision, locate multiple and possibly competing thesis statements in your draft.

Go through your draft and underline potential thesis statements (as we have done in the student's draft). View the presence of multiple, perhaps even competing, theses as an opportunity rather than a problem. In an exploratory draft, a range of interpretations of evidence constitutes raw material, the records of your thinking that might be developed in a more finished draft.

In the *Las Meninas* paper no single idea emerges clearly as the thesis. Instead, the writer has arrived (in paragraph 8) at three related but not entirely compatible ideas:

> "I think that Velázquez wants the king to . . ."
> **Thesis 1:** give Velázquez "the recognition he deserves by including him in the 'family.'"
> **Thesis 2:** "show that his [Velázquez's] status and brilliance [as an artist] have been appreciated."
> **Thesis 3:** give Velázquez "the credit he deserved for being a loyal friend and servant."

These three ideas about the painter's intentions could be made to work together, but at present the writer is left with an uneasy fit among them. In order to resolve the tension among her possible thesis statements, the writer appears to have settled on "*I think that Velazquez wants the king to give him the recognition he deserves by including him in the family.*" This idea follows logically from a number of the details the writer has focused on, so it is viable as a working thesis—the one that she will, in revision, test against potentially complicating evidence and evolve.

It helps that the writer has specified her *interpretive context*—the painter's intentions—because a writer's awareness of her interpretive context makes it much easier for her to decide which details to prioritize and what kind of questions to ask about them. A different interpretive context for the *Las Meninas* paper, such as the history of painting techniques or the social structure of seventeenth-century royal households, would have caused the writer to emphasize different details and arrive at different conclusions about their possible significance.

The success of analytical arguments often depends on a writer's ability to persuade readers of the appropriateness of her choice of interpretive context. And so it is important for writers to ask and answer the question "In what context might my subject best be understood and why?"

It is okay, by the way, that the writer has not concerned herself prematurely with organization, introductions, or transitions. She has instead allowed her draft to move freely from idea to idea as these occurred to her. She might not have come up with the useful ideas in paragraph 8 had she pressed herself to commit to any one idea (the divine right of kings idea, for example) too soon.

Notice that this writer has prompted a sequence of thought by using the word "*interesting*." Repeated use of this word as a transition would not be adequate in a final draft because it encourages listing without explicit connections among claims or explanations of how each claim evolved into the next. In an exploratory draft, however, the word "interesting" keeps the writer's mind open to possibilities and allows her to try on various claims without worrying prematurely about whether her tentative claims are right or wrong.

Step 2: Explain how the details you have focused on in the evidence lead to your working thesis.

The writer of the *Las Meninas* paper has offered at least some evidence in support of her working thesis, "Velázquez wants the king to give him the recognition he deserves by including him in the family." She notes the symbol on the painter's vest, for example, which she says might have been added later by the king to show that the painter's "status and brilliance have been appreciated." She implies that the painter's "confident stance" and "steady stare" also support her thesis. Notice, however, that she has not spelled out her reasons for making this connection between her evidence and her claim.

Nor has she corroborated her claim about this evidence with other evidence that could lend more support to her idea. Interestingly, the potential thesis statements advanced in paragraph 8 are not connected with the rather provocative details she has noted in paragraphs 6 and 7: that "Velázquez dominates the painting along with the little girl," that he "takes up the whole left side along with his gigantic easel," and that "the king and queen are not as visible as they might be" suggesting that "they are not always at the center where everyone would expect them to be."

In revision, the writer would need to find more evidence in support of her claim and make the links between evidence and claims more explicit. She would also need to tackle the complicating evidence that she leaves dangling in paragraphs 6 and 7, which takes us to Step 3.

Step 3: Locate evidence that is not adequately accounted for by the working thesis and pursue the implications of that evidence by repeatedly asking "SO WHAT?" Explain how and why these pieces of evidence complicate the working thesis.

This is a key step in evolving a thesis—pursuing the piece or pieces of evidence that do not clearly fit with the working thesis, explaining why they don't fit, and determining what their significance might actually be. For this purpose, the writer would need to zoom in on the details of her evidence that she describes in paragraphs 6 and 7 and ASK "SO WHAT?" about them.

- **So what** that there are size differences in the painting? What might large or small size mean?

- **So what** that the king and queen are small, but the painter, princess, and dwarf (another servant) are all large and fairly equal in size and/or prominence?

Proposed answer: Perhaps the king and queen have been reduced so that Velázquez can showcase their daughter, the princess.

Test of this answer: The size and location of the princess (center foreground) seem to support this answer, as does the princess being catered to by the ladies in waiting. But, if the painting is meant to showcase the princess, what is the point of the painter's having made himself so large?

Another possible answer: Perhaps the small size and lack of physical prominence of the king and queen are relatively unimportant, in which case, what matters is that they are a presence, always overseeing events (an idea implied but not developed by the writer in paragraph 6).

Test of this answer: Further support for this answer comes from the possibility that we are meant to see the king and queen as reflected in a mirror on the back wall of the painter's studio (an idea the writer mentions), in which case they would be standing in front of the scene depicted in the painting, literally overseeing events. There isn't much evidence against this answer, except, again, for the large size of the painter, and the trivializing implications of the king and queen's diminution, but these are significant exceptions.

Another possible answer: Perhaps the painter is demonstrating his own ability to make the king and queen any size—any level of importance—he chooses. The king and queen are among the smallest as well as the least visible figures in the painting. Whether they are being exhibited as an actual painting on the back wall of the painter's studio (a possibility the writer has not mentioned) or whether they appear as reflections in a small mirror on that back wall, they certainly lack stature in the painting in comparison with the painter, who is not only larger and more prominent than they are but also who, as the writer notes, "dominates the painting along with the little girl." The little girl is the princess, herself, and the supposed subject of the painting within the painting that Velázquez is working on.

Test: This answer about the painter demonstrating his control of the representation of the king and queen seems credible. It has the most evidence in its favor and the least evidence to contradict it. The writer would probably want to choose this idea and would need to reformulate her thesis to better accommodate it, which takes us to Step 4.

Step 4: Use your analysis of the complicating evidence to reformulate the thesis. Share with readers your reasons for moving from your initial claim to this reformulation.

On the basis of the writer's answers in Step 3, it would appear that rather than showcasing royal power, the painting showcases the painter's own power. This idea is not a clear fit with the writer's working thesis about the painter's intentions, that "Velazquez wants the king to give him the recognition he deserves by including him in the family." So, what should the writer do?

What she should not do is beat a hasty retreat from her working thesis. She should use the complicating evidence to qualify, rather than abandon, her initial idea, which did, after all, have some evidence in its favor. Good writing shares with readers the thinking process that carried the writer forward from one idea to the next.

The writer's evolved thesis would need to qualify the idea of the painter wishing to be recognized as a loyal servant and accepted as a member of the family (which are, themselves, not entirely compatible ideas), since there is evidence in the painting suggesting a more assertive stance on the part of Velázquez about the importance of painters and their art.

The writer is now ready to pursue the next step in the revision process: looking actively for other features of the painting that might corroborate her theory. This takes us to step 5, the last step the writer would need to go through before composing a more polished draft.

Step 5: Test the adequacy of the evolved thesis by repeating steps two, three, and four until you are satisfied that the thesis statement accounts for your evidence as fully and accurately as possible. The best test of a thesis is to see how much of the relevant evidence it can reasonably account for.

The need to find additional corroboration is especially pressing for this writer because her new thesis formulation that the painting demonstrates the artist's power—not just his brilliance and desire for recognition—suggests an interpretation of the painting that would be unusual for an era in which most other court paintings flattered royal figures by portraying them as larger than life, powerful, and heroic.

It is unlikely that any thesis will explain all of the details in a subject, but a reasonable test of the value of one possible thesis over another is how much of the relevant evidence it can explain. So the writer would try to apply her new thesis formulation to details in the painting that have not yet received much attention, such as the painter's paralleling himself with the large dwarf on the other side of the painting.

This pairing of dwarf and painter might initially seem to spell trouble for the new thesis about the painter demonstrating his power to frame the way the monarchs are represented. If it was, in fact, the painter's intention to have his power recognized, why would he want to parallel himself—in size, placement, and facial expression—with a dwarf who is, presumably, a fairly low-level servant of the royal household, unlike the *meninas*, who are the daughters of aristocrats? So What that the dwarf is paralleled with the painter?

The writer might argue that the dwarf suggests a visual pun or riddle, demonstrating that in the painter's world the small can be made large (and vice versa, in the case of the king and queen). No longer "dwarfed" by his subordinate role as court painter, Velázquez stands tall. If this reading is correct, and if it is true, as the writer suggests, that Prince Philip himself later had the honorary cross added to Velázquez's vest, we might assume that the king either entirely missed or was able to appreciate the painter's wit.

Similarly, another of the writer's key observations—that the painter "plays" with viewers' expectations—fits with the thesis that the painting asks for recognition of the artist's power, not just his loyal service. In subverting viewers' expectations both by decentering the monarchs and concealing what is on the easel, the painter again emphasizes his power, in this case, over the viewers (among whom might be the king and queen if their images on the back wall are mirror reflections of them standing, like us, in front of the painting). He is not bound by their expectations, and in fact appears to use those expectations to manipulate the viewers: he can make them wish to see something he has the power to withhold.

Step 6: Rewrite the draft into a more coherent and fuller analysis of evidence, while retaining for readers the "thesis trail"—the various steps that you went through along the way to formulating the thesis you ultimately choose.

It is tempting at the end of the exploratory writing process for the writer to simply eliminate all the ideas and analysis that did not support her final choice of thesis. Why should you include all six steps when you now know what the best version of your thesis is going to be?

Good analytical writing is collaborative. To a significant extent, good writing recreates for readers the thinking process that produced its conclusions. It shares with readers how a writer arrives at ideas, not just what the writer ultimately thinks. It takes readers along on a cognitive journey through the process of formulating and reformulating that results in a carefully qualified statement of ideas. Having made the trip, readers are more likely to appreciate the explanatory power of the most fully articulated statement of the thesis.

In a final draft, a writer can capture for readers the phases of thinking she went through by, for example, wording the thesis as a Seems to be about x claim (SEEMS TO BE ABOUT X, BUT IS REALLY—OR ALSO—ABOUT Y; see Chapter 5). This wording would allow the writer of the *Las Meninas* paper to share with readers the interesting shift she makes from the idea that the painting promotes the divine right of kings to the idea that it also endorses the power of the painter to cause people to see royalty in this light (a visual pun, as the light on the princess is actually produced by the painter's brush).

The writer could also set up a thesis that puts X in tension with Y, while granting some validity to both. In this case, X (the painter wanting to be recognized as a member of the family) would serve as back pressure to drive Y (the painter wanting to demonstrate, tongue-in-cheek, the power of painters).

In an inductively organized paper, you would begin with a working thesis somewhat closer to the final version of the thesis than was the case in the exploratory draft, but you would still take the readers along on your step-by-step journey to your conclusions. In a deductively organized paper, wherein the thesis must appear from the outset in something close to its full version, you would still be able to show your readers how your thinking evolved. The writer of the *Las Meninas* paper could do this by beginning with details that seem to obviously support the thesis (large size and prominence of the painter and his easel relative to the king and queen) and then move to details (such as the large dwarf) that readers would be less likely to connect with the thesis without her help.

Recognizing and Fixing Weak Thesis Statements

This closing section of the chapter provides a revision-oriented treatment of the five most common kinds of weak thesis statements. Typically, a weak thesis is an unproductive claim because it doesn't actually require further thinking or proof, as, for example, "An important part of one's college education is learning to better understand others' points of view" (a piece of conventional wisdom that most people would already accept as true, and thus not in need of arguing).

FIVE KINDS OF WEAK THESIS STATEMENTS

1. A thesis that makes no claim ("This paper examines the pros and cons of")

2. A thesis that is obviously true or a statement of fact ("Exercise is good for you")

3. A thesis that restates conventional wisdom ("Love conquers all")

4. A thesis that offers personal conviction as the basis for the claim ("Shopping malls are wonderful places")

5. A thesis that makes an overly broad claim ("Individualism is good")

Weak Thesis Type 1: The Thesis Makes No Claim

Problem Examples

> I'm going to write about Darwin's concerns with evolution in *The Origin of Species*.
>
> This paper addresses the characteristics of a good corporate manager.

Both problem examples name a subject and link it to the intention to write about it, but they don't make any claim about the subject. As a result, they direct neither the writer nor the reader toward some position or organizational plan. Even if the second example were rephrased as "This paper addresses why a good corporate manager needs to learn to delegate responsibility," the thesis would not adequately suggest why such a claim would need to be argued or defended. There is, in short, nothing at stake, no issue to be resolved.

Solution: Raise specific issues for the essay to explore.

Solution Examples

> Darwin's concern with survival of the fittest in *The Origin of Species* initially leads him to neglect a potentially conflicting aspect of his theory of evolution—survival as a matter of interdependence.
>
> The very trait that makes for an effective corporate manager—the drive to succeed—can also make the leader domineering and, therefore, ineffective.

Some disciplines expect writers to offer statements of method and/or intention in their papers' openings. Generally, however, these openings also make a claim: for example, "In this paper, I examine how Congressional Republicans undermined the attempts of the Democratic administration to legislate a fiscally responsible health care policy for the elderly," not "In this paper, I discuss America's treatment of the elderly."

Weak Thesis Type 2: The Thesis Is Obviously True or Is a Statement of Fact

Problem Examples

> The jean industry targets its advertisements to appeal to young adults.
>
> The flight from teaching to research and publishing in higher education is a controversial issue in the academic world. I will show different views and aspects concerning this problem.

A thesis needs to be an assertion with which it would be possible for readers to disagree.

In the second example, few readers would disagree with the fact that the issue is "controversial." In the second sentence of that example, the writer has begun to identify a point of view—that the flight from teaching is a problem—but her declaration that she will "show different views and aspects" is a broad statement of fact, not an idea. The phrasing of the claim is noncommittal and so broad that it prevents the writer from formulating a workable thesis.

> **Solution:** Find some avenue of inquiry—a question about the facts or an issue raised by them. Make an assertion with which it would be possible for readers to disagree.

Solution Examples

> By inventing new terms, such as "loose fit" and "relaxed fit," the jean industry has attempted to normalize, even glorify, its product for an older and fatter generation.

> The "flight from teaching" to research and publishing in higher education is a controversial issue in the academic world. As I will attempt to show, the controversy is based to a significant degree on a false assumption, that doing research necessarily leads teachers away from the classroom.

Weak Thesis Type 3: The Thesis Restates Conventional Wisdom

Problem Example

> "I was supposed to bring the coolers; you were supposed to bring the chips!" exclaimed ex-Beatle Ringo Starr, who appeared on TV commercials for Sun County Wine Coolers a few years ago. By using rock music to sell a wide range of products, the advertising agencies, in league with corporate giants such as Pepsi, Michelob, and Ford, have corrupted the spirit of rock and roll.

"Conventional wisdom" is a polite term for cultural cliché. Most clichés were fresh ideas once, but over time they have become trite, prefabricated forms of nonthinking. Faced with a phenomenon that requires a response, inexperienced writers sometimes resort to a small set of culturally approved "answers." Because conventional wisdom is so general and so commonly accepted, however, it doesn't teach anybody—including the writer—anything. Worse, because the cliché looks like an idea, it prevents the writer from engaging in a fresh exploration of his or her subject.

There is some truth in both of the preceding problem examples, but neither complicates its position. A thoughtful reader could, for example, respond to the advertising example by suggesting that rock and roll was highly commercial long before it colonized the airwaves. The conventional wisdom that rock and roll is somehow pure and honest while advertising is phony and exploitative invites the savvy writer to formulate a thesis that overturns these clichés. It could be argued that rock has actually improved advertising, not that ads have ruined rock—or, alternatively, that rock has shrewdly marketed idealism to gullible consumers. At the least, a writer committed to the original thesis would do better to examine what Ringo was selling—what he/wine coolers stand for in this particular case—than to discuss rock and advertising in such predictable terms.

Solution: Seek to complicate—see more than one point of view on—your subject. Avoid conventional wisdom unless you can qualify it or introduce a fresh perspective on it.

Solution Example

> While some might argue that the presence of rock and roll soundtracks in TV commercials has corrupted rock's spirit, this point of view not only misrepresents the history of rock but also ignores the improvements that the music has brought to the quality of television advertising.

Weak Thesis Type 4: The Thesis Bases Its Claim on Personal Conviction

Problem Examples

> Sir Thomas More's *Utopia* proposes an unworkable set of solutions to society's problems because, like communist Russia, it suppresses individualism.
>
> Although I agree with Jeane Kirkpatrick's argument that environmentalists and business should work together to ensure the ecological future of the world, and that this cooperation is beneficial for both sides, the indisputable fact is that environmental considerations should always be a part of any decision that is made. Any individual, if he looks deeply enough into his soul, knows what is right and what is wrong. The environment should be protected because it is the right thing to do, not because someone is forcing you to do it.

Like conventional wisdom, personal likes and dislikes can lead inexperienced writers into knee-jerk reactions of approval or disapproval, often expressed in a moralistic tone. The writers of the preceding problem examples assume that their primary job is to judge their subjects, or testify to their worth, not to evaluate them analytically. They have taken personal opinions for self-evident truths. (See Naturalizing Our Assumptions in Chapter 1.)

The most blatant version of this tendency occurs in the second problem example, which asserts, "Any individual, if he looks deeply enough into his soul, knows what is right and what is wrong. The environment should be protected because it is the right thing to do." Translation (only slightly exaggerated): "Any individual who thinks about the subject will obviously agree with me because my feelings and convictions feel right to me and therefore they must be universally and self-evidently true." Testing an idea against your own feelings and experience is not an adequate means of establishing whether something is accurate or true.

Solution: Try on other points of view honestly and dispassionately; treat your ideas as hypotheses to be tested rather than obvious truths. In the following solution examples, we have replaced opinions (in the form of self-evident truths) with ideas—theories about the meaning and significance of the subjects that are capable of being supported and qualified by evidence.

Solution Examples

Sir Thomas More's *Utopia* treats individualism as a serious but remediable social problem. His radical treatment of what we might now call "socialization" attempts to redefine the meaning and origin of individual identity.

Although I agree with Jeane Kirkpatrick's argument that environmentalists and business should work together to ensure the ecological future of the world, her argument undervalues the necessity of pressuring businesses to attend to environmental concerns that may not benefit them in the short run.

Weak Thesis Type 5: The Thesis Makes an Overly Broad Claim

Problem Examples

Violent revolutions have had both positive and negative results for man. *Othello* is a play about love and jealousy.

Overly generalized theses avoid complexity. Such statements usually lead either to say-nothing theses or to reductive either/or thinking. Similar to a thesis that makes no claim, theses with overly broad claims say nothing in particular about the subject at hand and so are not likely to guide a writer's thinking beyond the listing stage. One of the best ways to avoid drafting overly broad thesis statements is to sensitize yourself to the characteristic phrasing of such theses: "both positive and negative," "many similarities and differences," "both pros and cons." Virtually everything from meatloaf to taxes can be both positive and negative.

Solution: Convert broad categories and generic claims to more specific, more qualified assertions; find ways to bring out the complexity of your subject.

Solution Examples

Although violent revolutions begin to redress long-standing inequities, they often do so at the cost of long-term economic dysfunction and the suffering that attends it.

Although *Othello* appears to attack jealousy, it also supports the skepticism of the jealous characters over the naïveté of the lovers.

CHAPTER 8

Using Images to Make Meaning

We've just discussed, in a good deal of depth, the mechanics and rhetorical implications of bringing secondary sources into your paper. Now, as you deepen your thinking about your Symposium Presentation, you may well wonder whether there are similar rhetorical techniques for combining images with text.

And there are! But before we dive into discussing images specifically, let's take a moment to consider what happens structurally when you incorporate a secondary source into a research paper. Without any secondary sources, your paper is all of a piece: it's your writing, your thoughts—and that's all. Once you begin to bring in another person's thinking and writing, however, the paper becomes more complex: your thoughts and their thoughts jumble together on the page, interacting in interesting ways. Sometimes they support each other, sometimes they contradict each other, but the overall result is more complex and vibrant than any of the component pieces. It's almost like a textual mosaic, or collage.

In a very similar way, words can combine with images to make a collage of meaning. This opens up a wide array of possibilities, but when writers (even very experienced writers) begin to combine words and images, they often default to a simplistic relationship between the two. So, for example, someone writing about flowers might include an image of a generic flower. There's nothing wrong with this, exactly—all things else being equal, the image won't hurt the argument— but it's also not very interesting, because it's not adding anything to the message.

That's a shame, because images can do much more than merely illustrate the subject matter. Just as your thoughts can interact with another writer's in a variety of ways, so too can images expand your argument in unexpected and powerful ways. Scholars of rhetoric and of composition sometimes call this field of study *visual rhetorics*, and it's far too vast a subject for this chapter to cover entirely. By the end of this chapter, however, you should have an idea of the possibilities you can explore in your Symposium Presentation.

Before moving to more complex interactions between image and text, we need to establish a baseline. Returning to the idea of the flower above, let's say you wanted to include this sentence in a presentation: "From wildflowers to formal garden plantings, flowers provide texture and color to the human experience." This is a fairly bland statement, but an associated image might make it more interesting.

From wildflowers to formal garden plantings, flowers provide texture and color to the human experience.

Here, the bland statement is backed up by a similarly bland image. No one could argue with it—the pictured flowers do provide texture and color—but it's also a mere *illustration*. The image isn't really adding much to the words, other than a sort of decoration.

What if, instead, this were the combination:

From wildflowers to formal garden plantings, flowers provide texture and color to the human experience.

Many viewers will find the bright purple puffs of allium flowers more visually interesting than the bugleweeds in the first picture: they are a more unusual shape, and their color stands out more from the background. In addition, the photographer has adjusted the focus so that the front allium stands out crisply, and the others become more unfocused as they reduce into the blurry background. While the words discuss color and texture, the vibrant colors and enhanced textures of the image act as a *reinforcement*. The words seem to carry more weight, because they gain support from the image.

Images do not, however, always support the words they appear with:

From wildflowers to formal garden plantings, flowers provide texture and color to the human experience.

While the words speak about texture and color of actual flowers, this author has chosen to include a line drawing of a flower: not an actual flower at all, but instead an *abstraction*. At their best, abstractions can evoke a universal ideal and stand in as symbols for an entire group of actual things. At their worst, abstractions feel disconnected, as if the author didn't give much thought to their choice. (Tip: this negative reading tends to intensify with clip art, which often feels generic—because it is generic, by design. While you could certainly come up with a very good reason to use a piece of clip art, think carefully about whether your reader will get the impression you expect.)

Images can even directly contradict the words they accompany:

From wildflowers to formal garden plantings, flowers provide texture and color to the human experience.

While the words don't specifically talk about beauty or liveliness, they imply a positive feeling toward flowers. When combined with this picture of a withered daffodil bloom, they provoke a complex reaction in the reader: the words bring a positive impression of life and beauty, while the image brings ideas of death and ugliness. It's impossible to entirely predict how each reader will react, but the author can reasonably expect that their readers might muse on whether ugliness is also a form of texture and color, and even whether decline is also a part of the human experience. This kind of *contradiction* could be especially helpful to the author if they wish to explain these kinds of complex questions later in the presentation.

Images can also introduce entirely new arguments:

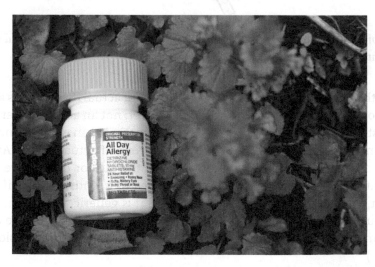

From wildflowers to formal garden plantings, flowers provide texture and color to the human experience.

Unlike the image of the dead flower, this image doesn't directly contradict the words it accompanies. There are, in fact, flowers pictured, and they
do provide both color and texture. But this image adds entirely new information to the argument: the bottle of allergy pills acts as an *expansion* of the
argument, making the reader consider not only the aesthetic consequences
of flowers, but also the physiological ones (namely, that flowers make some
people's eyes and noses run—quite a different sort of texture and color).
Depending on the overall message of the presentation, this expansion might
be useful, or it might be distracting.

Often images aren't so easy to typify as the ones above.

*From wildflowers to formal garden plantings, flowers provide texture and color
to the human experience.*

Here, the image shown is quite ambiguous. It's certainly an abstraction, like
the line drawing above. But the flower also seems to be drawn by spilling something powdery, like flour. It's hard to say what the purpose of this image is, in
the context of the words it appears with. Are readers supposed to recognize the
visual pun between 'flower' and 'flour'? Should they focus on the fact that the
'flower' is drawn on concrete, which could be thought of as a contradiction?
Should they consider the different textures (concrete, plastic cup, spilt flower)?
While ambiguous images like this one can be thought-provoking, they also run
the risk of distracting from the message of the presentation, since readers may
be too pre-occupied with their own questions to understand the message the
author is trying to convey.

This is only the tip of the iceberg, when it comes to the many ways words
and images combine to form meanings. (And this chapter doesn't even cover

the complexities that occur when multiple images appear simultaneously, since those images interact with each other and also with their accompanying words.) When you compose your Symposium Presentation—or another other, future multimedia project—remember that images can and should do a lot of the rhetorical heavy lifting. Just as you do when writing your Analytical Research Paper, think carefully about how best to craft your Symposium Presentation message using all the tools available: choose your images as carefully as your words.

CHAPTER 9

What is a Paper Supposed to Look Like?

Many students arrive in English 1110 with a narrowly limited idea of what an academic research paper is supposed to look like. They may have written examples of the well-known five-paragraph essay, or persuasive papers that required them to support a set thesis statement. Some students may have little experience writing research papers of any kind. With this in mind, it's useful to consider the broad form that an academic research paper is generally expected to take.

The Introduction

The introduction to an academic research paper is usually (though not always) one paragraph. It is the section in which the author explains to the audience why the paper is being written. In other words: what new, interesting, or significant idea is the author presenting in this paper?

In order to establish that this idea is new, interesting, or significant, the author may briefly summarize the context in which he or she is writing, including: a common assumption that is being challenged, a previous consensus that is being questioned, or an obvious conclusion that the paper seeks to contradict. There is no need to go into great detail here, and you should avoid stating your conclusion up front. Use the introduction not to tell the audience exactly what your paper is saying, but to identify for them why what you are going to say matters.

Common problems that authors encounter when writing introductions include: stating the conclusion (as we have already mentioned), providing so much background or detail that the audience is overwhelmed, attempting to introduce themes outside the scope of the paper, and deflating the importance of the paper by answering the central question that is asked—thereby removing any compelling reason for the audience to read the paper. *Writing Analytically* expands on a few of these typical problems:

Digression: Digression results when you try to include too much background. If, for example, you plan to write about a recent innovation in video technology, you'll need to monitor the amount and kind of technical information you include in your opening paragraphs. You'll also want to avoid starting at a point that is too far away from your immediate concerns, as in "From the beginning of time humans have needed to communicate."

As a general rule in academic writing, don't assume that your readers know little or nothing about the subject. Instead, use the social potential of the introduction to negotiate with your audience, setting up your relationship with your readers and making clear what you are assuming they do and do not know.

Incoherence: Incoherence results when you try to preview too much of your paper's conclusion in the introduction. Such introductions move in too many directions at once, usually because the writer is trying to conclude before going through the discussion that will make the conclusion comprehensible. The language you are compelled to use in such cases tends to be too dense, and the connections between the sentences tend to get left out, because there isn't enough room to include them. After having read the entire paper, your readers may be able to make sense of the introduction, but in that case, the introduction has not done its job.

The following introductory paragraph is incoherent, primarily because it tries to include too much. It neither adequately connects its ideas nor defines its terms.

> Twinship is a symbol in many religious traditions. The significance of twinship will be discussed and explored in the Native American, Japanese Shinto, and Christian religions. Twinship can be either in opposing or common forces in the form of deities or mortals. There are several forms of twinship that show duality of order versus chaos, good versus evil, and creation versus destruction. The significance of twinship is to set moral codes for society and to explain the inexplicable.

Prejudgment: Prejudgment results when you appear to have already settled the question to be pursued in the rest of the paper. The problem here is logical. In the effort to preview your paper's conclusion at the outset, you risk appearing to assume something as true that your paper will, in fact, need to test. In most papers in the humanities and social sciences, where the thesis evolves in specificity and complexity between the introduction and conclusion, writers and readers can find such assumptions prejudicial. Opening in this way, in any event, can make the rest of the paper seem redundant. Even in the sciences, in which a concise statement of objectives, plan of attack, and hypothesis are usually required up front, separate "Results" and "Discussion" sections are reserved for the conclusion.

In addition to the big-picture problems *Writing Analytically* notes, here are some tips to avoid other common mistakes inexperienced writers make in introductions:

- **An introduction should not begin at the dawn of history**. If you attempt to connect your paper to age-old questions that humankind has struggled with since the beginning of time, you are suggesting a scope that is far beyond that of an academic research paper! Your paper is probably not going to answer any age-old human questions, and that's perfectly okay.

- **An introduction should not include a dictionary definition.** While there are some exceptions to this rule, the use of a dictionary definition generally suggests that your paper is going to be dealing with the huge scope of a word's entire meaning. This is particularly true if the word is a broad, abstract concept like "justice" or "love." It's okay that the scope of your paper is more limited!

- **An introduction should accurately establish what your paper hopes to achieve.** If you suggest to the audience that you are about to reveal a particular kind of new, interesting, or significant idea, and then go on to write about an entirely different idea, this will damage your *ethos*. If you are struggling to communicate why the actual thesis of your paper matters, you may need to re-examine your thesis! We'll get to that in a moment, but first...

We've discussed what *not* to do, but what should a good introduction accomplish, and how can it do so? *Writing Analytically* also has tips on smart tactics to use in framing your essay:

Some Good Ways to Begin a Paper

All of the following ways to begin a paper enable you to play an ace, establishing your authority with your readers, without having to play your whole hand. They offer a starting position, rather than a miniaturized version of the entire paper. Remember that the aim of the introduction is to answer the question, Why does what I'm about to say matter? What makes it especially interesting or revealing, and in what context? Here are a few methods of accomplishing this aim.

CHALLENGE A COMMONLY HELD VIEW This move provides you with a framework against which to develop your ideas; it allows you to begin with some back pressure, which will help you to define your position. Because you are responding to a known point of view, you have a ready way of integrating context into your paper. As the economics professor notes of the FDR example, until we understand what the prevailing view is on FDR, it is pointless to start considering whether or not he was a Keynesian.

BEGIN WITH A DEFINITION Beginning with a definition is a reliable way to introduce a topic, so long as that definition has some significance for the discussion to follow. If the definition doesn't do any conceptual work in the introduction, the definition gambit becomes a pointless cliché.

You are most likely to avoid cliché if you cite a source other than a standard dictionary for your definition. The reference collection of any academic library contains a range of discipline-specific lexicons that provide more precise and authoritative definitions than Webster ever could. A useful alternative is to quote a particular author's definition of a key term because you want to make a point about his or her particular definition: for example, "Although the *Dictionary of Economics* defines Keynesianism as XYZ, Smith treats only X and Y (or substitutes A for Z, and so forth)."

LEAD WITH YOUR SECOND-BEST EXAMPLE Another versatile opening gambit, where disciplinary conventions allow, is to use your *second-best example* to set up the issue or question that you later develop in-depth with your best example. This gambit is especially useful in papers that proceed inductively on the strength of representative examples, an organizational pattern common in the humanities. As you are assembling evidence in the outlining and pre-writing stage, in many cases you will accumulate a number of examples that illustrate the same basic point. For example, several battles might illustrate a particular general's military strategy; several primaries might exemplify how a particular candidate tailors his or her speeches to appeal to the religious right; several scenes might show how a particular playwright romanticizes the working class; and so on.

Save the best example to receive the most analytical attention in your paper. If you were to present this example in the introduction, you would risk making the rest of the essay vaguely repetitive. A quick close-up of another example will strengthen your argument or interpretation. By using a different example to raise the issues, you suggest that the phenomenon exemplified is not an isolated case and that the major example you will eventually concentrate upon is, indeed, representative.

EXEMPLIFY THE TOPIC WITH A NARRATIVE The narrative opening, an occasional gambit in the humanities and social sciences, introduces a short, pertinent, and vivid story or anecdote that exemplifies a key aspect of a topic. Although generally not permissible in the formal reports assigned in the natural and social sciences, narrative openings turn up in virtually all other kinds of writing across the curriculum.

As the introduction funnels to its thesis, the readers receive a graphic sense of the issue that the writer will now develop nonnarratively. Nonnarrative treatment is necessary because by itself anecdotal evidence can be seen as merely personal. Storytelling is suggestive but usually does not constitute sufficient proof; it needs to be corroborated.

The Thesis Statement

The introduction to a paper typically includes a clear, concise, and interesting statement of the paper's thesis (as we have previously discussed). This thesis statement may be one or more sentences. It is more effective for a thesis statement to take the form of multiple clear sentences than for it to be confined to one long, unclear sentence.

Thesis development should be a core part of your writing process, since it shapes the entire purpose of your paper! However, it is important to remember that a thesis statement should also be *part* of your paper—not a separate block of text that has no connection to the sentences around it. Make sure that your introduction leads naturally into your thesis statement, and that you are not simply beginning your paper all over again once you have stated your thesis! To do this effectively, you will need to carefully consider exactly how much information to include in the introduction, as opposed to the paper itself.

How Much of the Thesis Belongs in the Introduction?

Once you have created the opening frame that leads to your thesis, you have choices about how much of your thesis to state at the outset and in what form. These choices are determined in some cases by the standard practices of the various academic disciplines. In some disciplines, for example, the introduction must offer a complete statement of the guiding claim. In many cases, this is done overtly with a procedural statement such as: "In this essay I will argue that . . ." This way of beginning is common not only in the natural and social sciences, but also in philosophy, art history, and in some other humanities disciplines. The procedural statement is sometimes followed by a roadmap that specifies the organization of the paper: "First A will be discussed, then B, etc." Such a detailed overview of a paper is not the norm, however, and is usually not necessary, especially in short essays.

To make your introduction sufficiently engaging and concrete, you should offer readers a brief preview of the particular details that led you to arrive at your thesis, or at least to the question that your thesis seeks to answer. Use these details to generate a theory, a *working hypothesis* about whatever you think is at stake in the material. As a general rule, assume that readers of your essay would need to know on page one, preferably by the end of your first paragraph or the beginning of the second, what your paper is attempting to resolve or negotiate. If you find yourself writing a page-long introductory paragraph to get to your initial statement of thesis, try settling for a simpler articulation of your central idea in its first appearance. Keep in mind that an introduction is not a conclusion. The opening claim is a hypothesis that the body of your paper will test. Your final assessment of the claim will appear in your paper's closing paragraphs.

In large and more complex pieces of thinking, though sometimes even in short ones, the introductory paragraph may be used to set up the first phase of the paper's discussion without having to frame and forecast the whole paper. Especially in inductively organized (specific to general) essays, where a full and complexly qualified articulation of the thesis becomes evident in stages, what you need is an opening claim sufficient to get the paper started. Begin with the best version of your thesis that you can come up with that will be understandable to your readers without a lengthy preamble. Set up this working thesis as quickly and concretely as you can, avoiding generic (fits anything) comments, throat clearing, and overblown historical claims ("Since the beginning of time, humans have been fascinated by technology . . ."). Once established, the working thesis will supply a relatively stable point to which you can return periodically for updating and to keep your readers (and yourself) on track.

Body Paragraphs: Evidence & Demonstrations

The majority of an academic research paper is made up of paragraphs that demonstrate the thesis of the paper. These paragraphs provide evidence for the central claim of the paper, laying out the author's argument in a logically organized and compelling manner that carries the reader from the beginning of the argument to its conclusion.

But what is a paragraph? You may have learned previously some specific metric, like "a paragraph has to have at least three sentences," or "a paragraph should have a beginning, middle, and end." Those metrics, however, don't really explain the underlying structure of a paragraph: what it does, not just what it looks like.

The Idea of the Paragraph

Throughout this section of the chapter, we will focus on what are sometimes called "body" paragraphs, as opposed to the more special-function paragraphs that serve as the beginnings and ends of papers.

It is useful to think of any piece of writing as consisting of parts or blocks. The paragraph is a fundamental building block, bigger than the sentence, smaller than the section or paper. Paragraphs can be thought of by analogy with the paper. Like papers, paragraphs have parts: they make opening gambits, they put forward evidence and analyze it, and they arrive at some kind of summarizing or culminating closure. They have, in short, a beginning, a middle, and an end. But unlike the paper, the paragraph does not stand alone as an independent entity. For a paragraph to be effective, readers need to be able to understand its role in unfolding the thinking of the paper as a whole.

The two primary characteristics of virtually all strong paragraphs are unity and development.

- **unity:** all the sentences in the paragraph should be related to some central idea or focus. Normally, the sentence that serves this function in the paragraph is the topic sentence.

- **development:** the sentences in a paragraph need to connect to each other in some way; a paragraph needs to go somewhere, to build. Normally, the sentences in a paragraph either offer a series of observations about the main idea or build one upon the next to offer a more sustained analysis of one element of the main idea.

Notice that we don't say here that a paragraph offers a claim plus examples and reasons. This model of the paragraph is true in some cases, but paragraphs typically do more than make simple claims and then back them up with one or more examples.

Once you begin paying attention to paragraphs, you will see that they are far less uniform in their shapes and procedures than you may have been taught to believe. The paragraph police will not haul you away for producing a paragraph that lacks a topic sentence, or places it at the end of the paragraph instead of the front, or contains several claims instead of one, or delays the substantiating evidence till later. Nonetheless, most of the paragraphs you encounter—and most that you should write—have unity and development. They are about one thing, and they tell you why it is important.

How Long?: Paragraphs, Readers, and Writers

Paragraphing is a kindness to your reader, since it divides your thinking into manageable bites. If you find a paragraph growing longer than half a page—particularly if it is your opening or second paragraph—find a place to make a paragraph break. More frequent paragraphing provides readers with convenient resting points from which to relaunch themselves into your thinking. In addition, paragraph indentations allow readers to scan essays, searching for connecting words and important ideas.

Long paragraphs are daunting for both readers and writers. When writers try to do too much in a single paragraph, they often lose the focus and lose contact with the larger purpose or point that got them into the paragraph in the first place. Remember that old rule about one idea to a paragraph? Well, it's not a bad rule, though it isn't exactly right because sometimes you need more space than a single paragraph can provide to lay out a complicated phase of your overall argument. In that case, just break wherever it seems reasonable to do so in order to keep your paragraphs from becoming ungainly. Two paragraphs can be about the same thing, the first half and then the second half. This paragraph, for example, might have been easier to process if we had broken it right before the question about that old rule.

A short paragraph will always provide emphasis, for which most readers will thank you.

Paragraphs are a relief not just for your readers: they also give the writer a break. When you draft, start a new paragraph whenever you feel yourself getting stuck: it's the promise of a fresh start. Paragraph breaks are like turning a corner to a new view, even when the thinking is continuous. They also force the writer to make transitions, overt connections among the parts of his or her thinking, and to state or restate key ideas.

It can be extraordinarily useful to draft a paper in phases, as a series of paragraphs:

- Break up the larger interpretation or argument into more manageable pieces.

- Give yourself space to think in short sections that you can then sequence.

- Clean up your thinking in revision by dividing its sections or phases into paragraphs.

Paragraphs need to justify their existence. A paragraph break should remind you to check that you have suggested to the readers why they need to know this information. Ask yourself why you are telling them what you are telling them. How does the thinking in the paragraph relate to the overall idea that your paper is developing? A good way to check if your paragraph is really advancing your claims is to ASK and answer "SO WHAT?" at the end of the paragraph.

Linking the Sentences in Paragraphs: Minding the Gaps

It helps to think of the space between the period at the end of a sentence and the beginning of the next sentence as a gap that the reader has to cross. Start thinking in this way as you follow the train of thought in this paragraph and those that follow it. Keep asking yourself: what is the connection between each sentence and the one that follows it? What keeps the reader from falling out of the paper at the gaps between sentences, losing sight of the thought connections that make a paragraph more than just a collection of sentences?

In many paragraphs, the connections between and among sentences are made apparent by the repetition of **key words**. This idea of key words brings us back to a core principle of this book: that both writers and readers make meaning by locating significant patterns of repetition and contrast. What is the pattern of repeated words in the paragraph above this one, for example? Notice the repetition of the key word "gap," which goes with the idea of falling and which is in opposition to such words as "connection" and "train of thought." The other connecting feature of the paragraph comes with its repeated use of questions. The paragraph you are now reading gets its sense of purpose from the previous paragraph's questions. Here we start answering them.

Sometimes (but not always) the connecting logic that helps readers negotiate the gaps between sentences must be made explicit. So, for example, some sentences begin with the words, "So, for example." The function of this type of connection is illustration. Some other words that operate in this gap-bridging way are "thus," "furthermore," "in addition," "similarly," "in other words," and "on the contrary."

When the organizing principle of a paragraph is sufficiently evident, explicit transitional words are often not needed. If parallelism is the paragraph's organizing principle, for example, readers will be able to see the relationship among the paragraph's sentences without a lot of repetition of connecting words.

The Shaping Force of Transitions

The linkage between where you've been and where you're going is usually a point in your writing at which thinking is taking place. This is especially the case in the evolving rather than the static model of thesis development, in which the writer continually *updates* the thesis as it moves through evidence.

- Thinking tends to occur at points of transition.
- A good transition articulates a paper's logical links—how each phase of the paper leads to the next.
- Too many additive transitions ("also," "another example of") produce papers that list, an overly loose form of organization

It is useful to think of transitions as *directional indicators*, especially at the beginnings of paragraphs but also within them. "And," for example, is a plus sign. It indicates that the writer will add something, continuing in the same direction. The words "but," "yet," "nevertheless," and "however" are among the many transitional words that alert readers to changes in the direction of the writer's thinking. They might indicate the introduction of a qualification, or a potentially contradictory piece of evidence, or an alternative point of view.

Some additive transitions do more work than "also" or "another." The word "moreover" is an additive transition, but it adds emphasis to the added point. The transitional sequence "not only . . . but also" restates and then adds information in a way that clarifies what has gone before.

Too many additive transitions can pose a problem for your writing. A list is a slack form of organization, one that fails to identify how this is related to that. Although transitional wording such as "another example of" or "also" at the beginning of paragraphs does tell readers that a related point or example will follow, it does not specify that relationship beyond piling on another "and." Essentially, these words just list.

If you find yourself relying on "another" and "also" at points of transition, force yourself to substitute other transitional wording that indicates more precisely the nature of the relationship with what has gone before in the paper. Language such as "similarly" and "by contrast" can sometimes serve this purpose. Often some restatement is called for to keep your reader on track—brief repetition is not necessarily redundant. A good transition reaches backward, telling where you've been, as the grounds for making a subsequent move forward.

The first step toward improving your use of transitions (and thereby, the organization of your writing) is to become conscious of them. If you notice that you are beginning successive paragraphs with "Another reason," for example, you can probably conclude that you are listing rather than developing your ideas. If you notice a number of sentences that start with the vague referent "This," you probably need to name the thing "This" refers to.

Think of transitions as echoes in the service of continuity. If you study the transitions in a piece, you will usually find that they echo either the language or the ideas of something that precedes them as they point to what is ahead.

The Conclusion

The conclusion to an academic research paper is typically—in a way that mirrors the introduction—one paragraph. In fact, the conclusion's similarities to the introduction go beyond the question of its size. The conclusion, like the introduction, is primarily concerned less with *what* the thesis of the paper is than with *why and how it matters*.

By the time you reach the conclusion of your paper, you have demonstrated your thesis. This being the case, your task is now to revisit what you established in the introduction: why your thesis is new, interesting, or significant. However, your conclusion should not simply restate ideas from your introduction. It is important to take into account that the audience has now read the entire paper. Therefore, their understanding of your thesis has expanded enormously. The audience is now prepared to consider complex questions about why and how your thesis matters.

For instance: does your thesis have implications beyond what you have discussed in the introduction? Are there troubling questions that your thesis points to? Does your thesis suggest larger problems that future work might address? These might all be areas that an effective conclusion explores.

What Conclusions Do: The Final "SO WHAT?"

Like the introduction, the conclusion has a key social function: it escorts the readers out of the paper, just as the introduction has escorted them in. The concluding paragraph presents the paper's final "SO WHAT?"

Conclusions always state the thesis in its most fully evolved form. In addition, the conclusion usually makes all of the following moves:

- *It comes full circle*. That is, it creates a sense of closure by revisiting the way the paper began. Often it returns to some key phrase from the context established in the introduction and updates it.

- *It pursues implications*. That is, it reasons from the particular focus of the essay to broader issues, such as the study's practical consequences or applications, or future-oriented issues, such as avenues for further research. To unfold implications in this way is to broaden the view from the here and now of the paper by looking outward to the wider world and forward to the future.

- *It identifies limitations*. That is, it acknowledges restrictions of method or focus in the analysis, and qualifies the conclusion (and its implications) accordingly.

These moves are quite literally movements—they take the thinking in the essay, and the readers with it, both backward and forward. The backward thrust we call *culmination*; the forward thrust we call *send-off*.

When you culminate a paper, you bring together things that you have already said, establishing their connection and ascending to one final statement of your thinking. The word "culminate" is derived from the Latin "*columen*," meaning "top or summit." To culminate is to reach the highest point, and it implies a mountain (in this case, of information and analysis) that you have scaled.

The climactic effects of culmination provide the basis for the send-off. The send-off is both social and conceptual, a final opening outward of the topic that leads the reader out of the paper with something further to think about. Here the thinking moves beyond the close analysis of data that has occupied the body of the paper into a kind of speculation that the writer has earned the right to formulate.

Simply put, you culminate with the best statement of your big idea, and your send-off gets you and the reader out of the paper.

Solving Typical Problems in Conclusions

The primary challenge in writing conclusions lies in finding a way to culminate your analysis without claiming either too little or too much. There are a number of fairly common problems to guard against if you are to avoid either of these two extremes.

Redundancy: In Chapter 4 we lampooned an exaggerated example of the five-paragraph form for constructing its conclusion by stating "Thus, we see" and then repeating the introduction verbatim. The result is redundancy. It's a good idea to refer back to the opening, but it's a bad idea just to reinsert it mechanically. Instead, reevaluate what you said there in light of where you've ended up, repeating only key words or phrases from the introduction. This kind of selective repetition is a desirable way of achieving unity and will keep you from making one of two opposite mistakes—either repeating too much or bringing up a totally new point in the conclusion.

Raising a Totally New Point: Raising a totally new point can distract or bewilder a reader. This problem often arises out of a writer's praiseworthy desire to avoid repetition. As a rule, you can guard against the problem by making sure that you have clearly expressed the conceptual link between your central conclusion and any implications you may draw. An implication is not a totally new point but rather one that follows from the position you have been analyzing.

Similarly, although a capping judgment or send-off may appear for the first time in your concluding paragraph, it should have been anticipated by the body of your paper. Conclusions often indicate where you think you (or an interested reader) may need to go next, but you don't actually go there. In a paper on the economist Milton Friedman, for example, if you think that another economist offers a useful way of critiquing him, you probably should not introduce this person for the first time in your conclusion.

Overstatement: Many writers are confused over how much they should claim in the conclusion. Out of the understandable (but mistaken) desire for a grand (rather than a modest and qualified) culmination, writers sometimes overstate the case. They assert more than their evidence has proven or even suggested. Must a conclusion arrive at some comprehensive and final answer to the question that your paper has analyzed?

Depending on the question and the disciplinary conventions, you may need to come down exclusively on one side or another. In a great many cases, however, the answers with which you conclude can be more moderate. Especially in the humanities, good analytical writing seeks to unfold successive layers of implication, so it's not even reasonable for you to expect neat closure. In such cases, you are usually better off qualifying your final judgments, drawing the line at points of relative stability.

Anticlimax: The end of the conclusion is a "charged" site, because it gives the reader a last impression of your paper. If you end with a concession—an acknowledgment of a rival position at odds with your thesis—you risk leaving the reader unsettled and possibly confused. The term for this kind of letdown is "anticlimax." In most cases, you will flub the send-off if you depart the paper on an anticlimax.

There are many forms of anticlimax besides ending with a concession. If your conclusion peters out in a random list or an apparent afterthought or a last-minute qualification of your claims, the effect is anticlimactic. And for many readers, if your final answer comes from quoting an authority in place of establishing your own, that, too, is an anticlimax.

A useful rule for the introduction is to play an ace but not your whole hand. In the context of this card-game analogy, it is similarly effective to save an ace for the conclusion. In most cases, this high card will provide an answer to some culminating "so WHAT?" question—a last view of the implications or consequences of your analysis.

APPENDIX 1

Grammar and Punctuation

Very often, writers arrive at college with a belief that there exists one "correct" form of English, and that their goal as students is to master this correct English. Many writers may have been previously told by teachers or textbooks that the English they use on an everyday basis is incorrect, and that learning an unchanging set of grammatical rules will allow them to "fix" this English.

The truth, however, is that there is no correct English. There is no unchanging set of grammatical rules that dictates how English sentences "should" operate. Rather, what counts as correct English is decided by a number of factors. For instance: who is speaking and to whom? Where is the conversation taking place? When is the conversation taking place? What is its purpose? (You may recognize these as rhetorical considerations!)

The English that you will be asked to write in this course is standard academic English. It conforms to certain conventions and expectations about what sentences will look like and how words will be used. In asking you to fulfill these conventions and expectations, our aim is not necessarily to make your writing "correct." In fact, while this appendix will use the terms "correct" and "incorrect" for simplicity's sake, we don't mean to suggest that there's one universally correct standard for writing. When we say 'correct', we mean correct for this style of writing, in this class (and in most other university classes). Our goal is to help you create writing that is easily understood and to allow you to present yourself as a skillful, competent communicator who ought to be taken seriously by the university community.

In this chapter, we also want to help you develop a more nuanced vocabulary to talk about your writing with your teacher and peers. Students come to the study of English with a variety of skills, struggles, confusions, and goals. Acquiring the ability to formulate and ask specific, meaningful questions will help you to understand your own struggles, resolve your own confusions, and, ultimately, achieve your own goals.

What we have presented here are some of the areas of confusion that are not only most common, but that also have the most significant impact—those areas of confusion, in other words, that are likely to prevent your writing from being understood clearly or that may impact your *ethos* as a writer if they are not addressed.

Sentence Fragments

A sentence fragment is exactly what it sounds like: a partial sentence. Sometimes a particular situation calls for a fragment—advertising copy, for example, thrives on fragments, as does dialogue in movies and books—but fragments are very rare in academic writing. That doesn't mean they never happen, but when they do it's for a particular rhetorical purpose that should be evident to a reader.

More commonly, inexperienced writers use sentence fragments in accidental ways that are confusing, because the sentence fragment can't stand on its own. It's missing some vital part of a complete sentence, and in order to do its job—that is, in order to communicate meaning to the reader—it must be completed with other pieces. In order to complete a sentence fragment, you will need to identify the parts that it is missing.

In order to understand what a complete sentence is, you need to learn about *clauses*. Clauses contain a **subject** (someone or something that is doing the action) and a **predicate** (the action, which includes a verb). Sentences can contain a single clause—"Dinosaurs are awesome."—but they can also contain multiple clauses linked together in particular ways to make complex thoughts. This is where inexperienced writers run into problems.

Clauses come in two main types: *independent* and *dependent*. *Independent clauses* can stand on their own; they are complete sentences by themselves. But what does that mean? To really understand it, you have to understand what a *dependent clause* is. Dependent clauses, well, *depend* on another clause. They are usually extra bits of information that are added to the main, independent clause: "Dinosaurs, *which are sadly now extinct*, are awesome." Try this: imagine walking up to someone out of the blue and just saying "which are now extinct." It doesn't really mean anything, because its meaning depends on the independent clause it's attached to, "Dinosaurs are awesome." (This trick doesn't always work, but it's a good guide.)

Incorrect:

1. A book filled with wonderful tales of dinosaurs and robots.
2. Including several histories of the Third Robot-Dinosaur War.
3. While it would be incorrect to describe this book as a masterpiece.
4. Especially when bookstores are filled with many excellent biographies of our first robot president.
5. Having failed in the their quest for both the White House and world domination.
6. The dinosaurs, who retreated to their wondrous space fortress.

Correct:

1. This book is filled with wonderful tales of dinosaurs and robots.
   The original fragment was only a subject. One solution is to provide it with a simple verb: here, the verb is.

2. The book is filled with wonderful tales, including several histories of the Third Robot-Dinosaur War.
   The original fragment is a dependent clause. One solution is to supply a main (independent) clause. Here, "including..." modifies the "tales" in the independent clause.

3. While it would be incorrect to describe this book as a masterpiece, it is certainly very entertaining.
   The original fragment is a dependent clause. The word while *should serve as a signal that this clause needs to be contrasted with an independent clause.*

4. Bookstores are filled with many excellent biographies of our first robot president.
   The original fragment is a dependent clause. One solution is to make it into an independent clause by removing the words Especially when, *which depend on another clause.*

5. Having failed in their quest for both the White House and world domination, the dinosaurs retreated.
   The original fragment is a dependent clause. Here, the independent clause the dinosaurs retreated *gives it something to modify.*

6. The dinosaurs, who retreated to their wondrous space fortress, soon decided to form their own independent nation.
   The original fragment lacks a predicate. Here, we have provided the dinosaurs *(the subject) with an action (soon decided to form their own independent nation).*

Subject-Verb Agreement

It is important for the subject and the verb in a sentence to match in *number*. Both the subject and the verb signal to the reader whether an action is being performed by *one* person (or thing) or *many* persons (or things). If the subject and the verb do not send the same signal, your reader will probably be confused.

Problems with mismatched subjects and verbs become are more common in longer, more complex sentences. The more clauses are combined to express complicated thoughts, the easier it is to lose track of the original subject, and instead to match the verb with the nearest noun.

While writers most often encounter these problems of subject-verb agreement in long, complicated sentences, these problems also occur with subject nouns that are modified by prepositional phrases. This can lead to a situation in which the subject is singular, but the noun closest to the verb is plural—or vice versa—as in several of the sentences below.

Incorrect:

1. The popularity of unusual flavors of ice cream cones have been increasing all across the country.

2. Each of the new flavors of ice cream cone offer a fantastical new journey for your taste buds.

3. Many new ingredients, such as corn, cheddar cheese, and olive oil, has become trendy and stylish.

4. Of course, none of the inhabitants of Ohio are surprised to learn that people like corn and cheddar cheese!

Correct:

1. The popularity of unusual flavors of ice cream cones has been increasing all across the country.
   The subject of this sentence is "popularity," which is singular. Therefore, you need a singular verb: has been. (Tip: try reading sentences without the prepositional phrase: "The popularity … has been increasing…")

2. Each of the new flavors of ice cream cone offers a fantastical new journey for your taste buds.
   "Each" is a shorter way of saying "each one," which is the singular subject of this sentence. It requires a singular verb: offers.

3. Many new ingredients, such as corn, cheddar cheese, and olive oil, have become trendy and stylish.
   The subject of this sentence is Many new ingredients, and it needs a plural verb: have become.

4. Of course, none of the inhabitants of Ohio is surprised to learn that people like corn and cheddar cheese!
   "None" is a shorter way of saying "not one," which is a singular subject. It needs a singular verb: is.

Comma Splices & Fused Sentences

Fused Sentences

Fused sentences (also sometimes called 'run-on sentences') are sentences in which two or more independent clauses have been jammed together without the appropriate punctuation, resulting in a confusing sentence that appears to have too many subjects (people or things) and predicates (actions).

The solution to a fused sentence is to break it up in a way that makes it clear, logical, and grammatical. You may do this by separating the independent clauses into different sentences, by inserting an appropriate conjunction and a comma, or—in some cases—by inserting a semicolon. Semicolons are most often appropriate when two independent clauses are very closely related, but it seems better not to have the interruption of a conjunction. It is often tempting for inexperienced writers to overuse semicolons; a wiser approach is to use them infrequently.

Incorrect:

1. The robots and the dinosaurs made a historic truce the world began a new and more peaceful era.

2. I watched as the president of the robots and the lord high emperor of the dinosaurs shook hands they seemed overcome by emotion.

3. Because he was a *Tyrannosaurus rex*, the lord high emperor of the dinosaurs had very tiny arms the president of the robots struggled to reach them.

Correct:

1. The robots and the dinosaurs made a historic truce, and the world began a new and more peaceful era.
   Each of these independent clauses can be a separate sentence, but they can also be joined by a comma and a conjunction.

2. I watched as the president of the robots and the lord high emperor of the dinosaurs shook hands. They seemed overcome by emotion.
   Here the two independent clauses make most sense when each is a separate sentence.

3. Because he was a *Tyrannosaurus rex*, the lord high emperor of the dinosaurs had very tiny arms; the president of the robots struggled to reach them.
   You could make each of these clauses a separate sentence. Here is another option: because the second clause logically follows the first, you can use a semicolon to separate them.

Comma Splices

In science and in science fiction, the word "splice" is sometimes used to describe a way of artificially or unnaturally linking two things together—for instance: rope, DNA strands, or fiber optic cables.

A comma splice is also a way of linking two things together, but one that isn't allowed by standard academic English: it is when two independent clauses are joined by a mere comma, instead of being separated into two sentences or joined using other, more substantial punctuation. By splicing these clauses together with a comma, you may think that you have avoided a fused sentence, but comma splices aren't allowed by the conventions of standard academic English. This is an arbitrary rule, but that's how it is.

Generally, comma splices can be fixed in the similar method to fused sentences: by replacing the comma with another punctuation mark, by adding a conjunction, or by using a semicolon where appropriate.

Incorrect:

1. A group of robots and a group of dinosaurs performed traditional folk dances to symbolize the unity of their two nations, the dances were very beautiful.

2. Robots and dinosaurs played Moog synthesizers and bagpipes, these instruments are often considered the cultural emblems of the two groups.

3. The robots and dinosaurs cheered, we all celebrated the fact that the war was over.

Correct:

1. A group of robots and a group of dinosaurs performed traditional folk dances to symbolize the unity of their two nations. The dances were very beautiful.

   You can easily separate these independent clauses into separate sentences.

2. Robots and dinosaurs played Moog synthesizers and bagpipes; these instruments are often considered the cultural emblems of the two groups.

   You can join these clauses with a semicolon. You could also turn each of them into a separate sentence.

3. The robots and dinosaurs cheered, and we all celebrated the fact that the war was over.

   Again, it is perfectly fine to turn each of these clauses into a separate sentence. However, you can also join them by adding a conjunction, as we have shown above.

The Possessive Apostrophe

A long time ago, in an England far, far away, the English language used to add letters—usually an e and an s—onto the end of a word in order to make it possessive. So, for instance, if you had a dragon and you wanted to indicate that it belonged to the king, you would say that it was the *kinges dragon*. Over time, English speakers began to skip saying the extra syllable this caused, in the same way that many modern English speakers say *y'all* instead of *you all*. The e was replaced by an apostrophe. Instead of *kinges dragon*, the phrase became *king's dragon*.

Incorrect:

The kings dragon was so badly trained that it set fire to the kingdom.

In this example, the writer has not actually told the reader that the dragon belongs to the king. Because there is no apostrophe, the word king is not possessive here.

Correct:

> The king's dragon was too well-trained to set fire to the kingdom.
> *The apostrophe tells you that the word king is possessive, and that the well-trained dragon belongs to the king.*

The question of how to show that a plural noun is possessive can seem more complicated, since the placement of the apostrophe depends on whether or not the plural noun ends in the letter s. If the plural noun does *not* end in the letter s, the apostrophe goes before the s. If the plural noun *does* end in the letter s, the apostrophe goes after the s.

The children's dragons defeated the kings' dragons in mortal combat.

There is a simple way to understand this rule if you remember that English speakers like to skip syllables whenever they can, just as we pointed out with *y'all* and *you all*. Think about how tricky it would be to have to talk about *the kings's dragons's teeth* and *the kings's dragons's claws*! That's a lot of extra syllables. It's much easier to drop the last s. So, instead, we have *the kings' dragons' teeth* and *the kings' dragons' claws*.

You can see how easy it can be to confuse your reader with misplaced possessive apostrophes. You will want to make sure that you have carefully considered what you are telling your reader—how many kings and how many dragons are you talking about?

One Very Confusing Exception This exception has to do with the tricky little word *it*. It causes problems because it already has a form that requires an apostrophe: *it's*, which means it is. You can see that the exact same rule about skipping syllables applies here: the apostrophe is replacing the i in is. So what happens when you want to talk about a dragon that belongs to it? How can you prevent your reader from being very confused?

The answer is that the possessive form of it does not have an apostrophe.

Incorrect:

> When the kingdom of Atlantis sank below the ocean, it's dragons all moved to Miami Beach.
> *Here, you are saying "it is dragons all moved to Miami Beach." This doesn't make any sense, and some readers will object!*

Correct:

> When the kingdom of Atlantis sank below the ocean, its dragons all moved to Miami Beach. It's unknown whether they wanted to play beach volleyball or if they just wanted to get a suntan.
> *"Its dragons" tells you that the dragons in question belonged to Atlantis. "It is unknown" what the goals of the dragons were.*

Homophones

Homophones are sets of words that sound the same as each other, even though they are often spelled differently. The prefix *homo-* literally means "same," and *phone* has to do with sound or voice. (Think of headphones!)

It is important to make sure that you know the correct spelling of the word you are using, and do not confuse it with another word that sounds the same. This is doubly true because the 'wrong' word is still a real word, so spellcheck won't notice it. Unfortunately, there's no easy way to deal with these; you just have to learn them.

Some examples of commonly confused homophones include:

two, to, and *too*

there, their, and *they're*

site, cite, and *sight*

write and *right*

bite and *byte*

morning and *mourning*

bow and *bough*

affect and *effect*

then and *than* (in some accents)

Even the most experienced writers often confuse homophones, particularly when they are tired or not being careful. The best strategy is to carefully proof-read your writing, paying close attention to any potential homophones.

Misplaced Modifiers & Dangling Participles

In English, word order is very important. Putting the words of an English sentence into a different order will create a radically different sentence! For instance, *The man wears a hat* has a very different meaning from *The hat wears a man*, and *The wears a hat man* is not even a meaningful English sentence at all.

A misplaced modifier is a problem of word order. Specifically, it is a problem that occurs when a word or a group of words that is intended to modify another word (a *modifier*) is separated from the word it is intended to modify. This means that the reader cannot always easily connect these words, and may misunderstand the sentence—sometimes to a very extreme degree! Misplaced modifiers can be hard to spot, because our brain autocorrects the error—we know what the writer meant—but properly placed modifiers make your writing feel more polished.

Incorrect:

1. Smothered in sour cream, guacamole, and jalapeños, I drooled over the plate of nachos.

2. Over spring break, I toured Miami Beach and took a photo of a shark in a double decker bus.
3. After devouring their nachos, the groovy waves seemed inviting to the surfers.
4. Surfers cruised the tasty waves, drinking colorful piña coladas on surfboards.

Correct:

1. I drooled over the plate of nachos, which were smothered in sour cream, guacamole, and jalapeños.
   In the incorrect example, smothered in sour cream, guacamole, and jalapeños is modifying I, not the nachos, so it sounds like the speaker is very messy!

2. Over spring break, I toured Miami Beach in a double decker bus and took a photo of a shark.
   Unless you met a shark in a double decker bus, this is the less confusing option!

3. After the surfers had devoured their nachos, the groovy waves seemed inviting.
   Was it the surfers or the groovy waves who devoured the nachos in the incorrect sentence?

4. Surfers cruised the tasty waves on surfboards, drinking colorful piña coladas.
   As delightful as the image of piña coladas on tiny surfboards of their own might be, this is probably closer to the intended meaning.

Sometimes, you may run into another problem with a modifier: the word it is intended to modify may not actually be in the sentence! It is surprisingly easy for even experienced writers to accidentally omit a key word or phrase.

Incorrect:

1. Surfing the tasty waves, a shark photobombed his vacation snapshot.
2. While whale-watching on a cruise, her sunglasses slipped into the ocean.

Correct:

1a. While he was surfing the tasty waves, a shark photobombed his vacation snapshot.
   or

1b. Surfing the tasty waves, he saw a shark photobomb his vacation snapshot.
   Either of these options provides the absent he that is meant to be modified by surfing the tasty waves. This prevents the reader from assuming that the shark is the one surfing the tasty waves!

2. While she was whale-watching on a cruise, her sunglasses slipped into the ocean.

This option provides the she that you need to use in order to clarify that her sunglasses were not whale-watching on a cruise.

The best way to guard against misplaced modifiers and dangling participles is to pay careful attention to your sentences. Make sure you understand how your words are working and which order will make the sentence clearest for the reader. Tip: the vast majority of the time, a modifier modifies the noun it's closest to.

Pronoun Agreement

A pronoun is a word that you use to replace a noun, often when using a noun would be repetitive or clumsy. For instance, instead of saying, "When velociraptors appear in dinosaur films, velociraptors are often shown to be extremely clever and even witty, despite the fact that dinosaur experts believe velociraptors to have been nothing of the sort," you might say: "When velociraptors appear in dinosaur films, they are often shown to be extremely clever and even witty, despite the fact that dinosaur experts believe them to have been nothing of the sort." In that sentence, "they" and "them" are pronouns that replace the noun "velociraptors." By using pronouns, you avoid creating a sentence that is so full of "velociraptors" that it becomes difficult to read.

English has three "persons" of pronoun: first person (I/me/we/us), second person (you), and third person (he/she/it/they/them). The person of the pronoun is determined by the person or thing it is replacing. For instance, "velociraptors," in the above sentence, is replaced by "they" and "them" because it is a plural noun that is neither the speaker of the sentence (the first person) nor the person being spoken to (the second person). Each of these three persons of pronoun also has possessive forms: my/mine/our/ours in the first person, your/yours in the second person, and his/her/hers/its/their/theirs in the third person.

All of these words are familiar to you, and you use them continually when you speak in English. However, in spite of this familiarity, pronouns are a frequent cause of confusion and problems for writers. There are several major sources of pronoun-related struggles.

Gender-neutral singular pronoun

In English, if you want to refer to a group of people who may be of any gender, you simply use the plural pronoun *they*. *They* refers to a group of people, without indicating gender.

However, traditionally English only has three basic singular pronouns: *he*, *she*, and *it*. *He* and *she* are implicitly gendered: they refer to a man and a woman, respectively. This is usually fine, but you may have become frustrated in the past when trying to write a sentence that requires a singular pronoun to refer to a person, but which doesn't specify the gender of the person in question. For instance, if you write a sentence such as, "An English teacher will inevitably make a pronoun error at some point in [pronoun] life," what is the correct pronoun to use? The gender of *an English teacher* is not clear, and it is therefore unclear whether *she* or *he* would be more accurate.

In the past, writers would typically use the pronoun *he* in all situations such as this. However, this practice is now widely viewed as unacceptably sexist: why would you assume that the English teacher in the example above was male? For similar reasons of limited representation, using *she* in these cases isn't common, either (though certain writers do go this route for political or ideological reasons). The only other traditionally singular pronoun is *it*, but *it* refers to inanimate objects, and cannot generally refer to people.

There are two major ways that people resolve the problem of a gender-neutral singular pronoun. Before we describe them, however, we wish to be clear that this is a question of grammar that is very much in flux in the public sphere, so you'll hear a variety of opinions on the matter in the news and in the classroom.

The first way some writers resolve the problem is to use *s/he* or *he or she* as an alternative option. This allows the possibility that the person in question is either female or male. So, you could opt to write "An English teacher will inevitably make a pronoun error at some point in *his or her* life." This tactic, however, can lead to rather wordy sentences, especially when it continues at length. It also ignores the possibility of the person being neither male nor female—we'll discuss this below.

The other major option is to use *they* as a gender-neutral singular pronoun—that is, "An English teacher will inevitably make a pronoun error at some point in *their* life." Although this usage, commonly called "singular they," has always been common in speech, it has traditionally not been considered standard professional or academic usage. However, as of 2015, major newspapers such as the *Washington Post* have endorsed this usage in their style guides, and the American Dialect Society voted 'singular they' its Word of the Year 2015. We, the writers of this book, endorse this change (and use it in this book): it's simple, it's concise, and it has a long history in English writing, including the works of great writers like William Shakespeare and Jane Austen.

The question of using *they* as a singular pronoun for an unknown person is often conflated with another important social issue: some individuals do not identify as either male or female, and prefer not to use *he* or *she* as their personal pronoun, as neither is correctly descriptive. The two issues are separate, but allowing for the unknown-person singular they also allows us to more respectfully include all members of our communities.

However, students need to be aware that this issue is far from settled, and many instructors may strongly disagree with using singular *they*. Therefore, the best practice for students is to be aware that change is ongoing in this area, and that individual teachers may differ in their preferences and expectations. One wise move may be to entirely sidestep the issue by rephrasing your sentence so that you can use a plural pronoun. For instance: "An English teacher will inevitably make a pronoun error at some point in [pronoun] life," becomes "*English teachers* will inevitably make pronoun errors at some point in *their* lives." Controversy avoided.

Unclear Pronouns

A sentence may sometimes be written in such a way that the reader has a difficult time understanding which noun a pronoun seems to be replacing. The simplest and most reliable way to prevent this problem is to carefully read and reread your own work, making sure that each pronoun can be matched with some previously stated noun (or *antecedent*).

Here are some examples of unclear pronoun usage:

Unclear:

1. The Tsar of All Russia had a magnificent dog before they sent him into space.

2. The practice of sending dogs into space was once very common, and several dog cosmonauts became celebrated heroes in the Soviet Union. However, as the Space Race ended, this changed.

3. Because dog cosmonauts were an emblem of the magic of technology and an adorable future in which dogs would travel through outer space, they became less popular when people lost interest in this.

Clearer:

1. The Tsar of All Russia had a magnificent dog before the Russian space agency sent the dog into space.
   There are two problems here: it is unclear to whom "they" refers, since no plural or gender-unspecified noun has been introduced, and "him" could refer to either the Tsar of All Russia or the Tsar's dog.

2. The practice of sending dogs into space was once very common, and several dog cosmonauts became celebrated heroes in the Soviet Union. However, as the Space Race ended, this practice changed.
   In the original sentence, it is unclear what "this" refers to: the practice of sending dogs, or their celebration. (Tip: if you find yourself writing 'this is', consider whether you need to specify what 'this' is.)

3. Because dog cosmonauts were an emblem of the magic of technology and an adorable future in which dogs would travel through outer space, they became less popular when people lost interest in these ideas.
   In the original sentence, it is not clear whether "this" refers to "the magic of technology," "an adorable future," or some combination of the two.

Too Many Commas, Not Enough Commas

Ah, the comma: the most controversial punctuation mark in the English language. Where does the comma go? Do you need a comma? Is the comma optional? Does anyone know?

The truth is that there are places where commas are required; where they're forbidden; and where they're optional, as a matter of stylistic preference. Fortunately, there are rules about all of these; unfortunately, comma usage is one of the most complex areas of English grammar. We'll try to highlight some major examples of the first two categories—instances when using or not using a comma will significantly impact the clarity of your sentence.

Required Commas

The clearest set of required commas is the set of commas that surrounds what is formally called a "nonrestrictive element," but which you might think of as the bonus materials of your sentence. In other words, a nonrestrictive element is a part of the sentence you could remove without affecting the structure of the rest of the sentence. For example: "Elvis Presley, who supposedly died in 1977, was recently spotted in Texas rustling longhorn cattle." If you remove the part of this sentence that is surrounded by commas ("who supposedly died in 1977") you will still have a perfectly reasonable sentence left: "Elvis Presley was recently spotted in Texas rustling longhorn cattle." Since the information about Elvis's death isn't necessary to the sentence, it should be set off with commas.

Another set of required commas are those that must come before a conjunction in a compound sentence—that is, a sentence that contains two independent clauses. (See **Comma Splices & Run-On Sentences** for more discussion.)

The last common required comma is the one that separates items in a list. You may have heard of the Oxford comma—the most famous comma in English, and certainly the only comma ever to have had a popular rock song named after it. This is the comma that separates items in a list from a conjunction. There's a great deal of disagreement among copy editors and writers about exactly what to do with list commas: do I write "apples, oranges, and pears" or "apples, oranges and pears"? (Yes, people really do have vicious fights about this. Strange but true.) If you go searching on the internet, you can find many articles, tweets, memes, etc. that argue one way or the other, claiming ambiguity in one case and clarity in the other.

The truth is that either usage—with the Oxford comma or without it—can both cause and alleviate confusion. The important thing is consistency: if you use the Oxford comma, *always* use the Oxford comma. If you don't, never do.

Here are some examples of comma problems and their solutions:

Unclear:

1. We went shopping for party supplies, a fish tank and twelve live eels.

2. The eels who had very angry expressions amused us greatly.
3. We cruised down the highway with our car full of eels and cows along the highway mooed as we passed.

Clearer:
1. We went shopping for party supplies, a fish tank, and twelve live eels.
   This is an example of a list where the Oxford comma doesn't appear. Many Oxford partisans would argue that this is confusing—that it implies that your party supplies were, in fact, "a fish tank and twelve live eels"—but in all likelihood the reader will understand if you've been consistent in your usage.

2. The eels, who had very angry expressions, amused us greatly.
   Let us assume that all of the eels were displeased about being in the fish tank. In that case, the information about angry expressions is a bonus: we don't need it. Therefore, it should be set off with commas.

3. We cruised down the highway with our car full of eels, and cows along the highway mooed as we passed.
   The original sentence creates a moment of confusion for the reader: it is unclear at first that "cows" are the subject of a new clause, and therefore it seems to the reader as though the eels and the cows are cruising down the highway with the writer. There needs to be a comma before 'and,' because it is the conjunction joining two independent clauses.

Forbidden Commas

You may have heard that "you should put a comma wherever you would take a breath." This leads to a good deal of extra commas, including ones that actually create confusion. While commas *may* sometimes occur in the places where a reader would naturally pause, there are many cases in which inserting commas where they should not go can damage your *ethos* and/or confuse your reader.

Previously, we described nonrestrictive elements as the "bonus material" added into your sentence. This bonus material can be removed from the sentence without affecting the sentence's overall sense and generally is enclosed by commas. However, *restrictive* material—material that is essential to the sense of your sentence—should *not* be set off or enclosed by commas. Let's say that in your zeal for eels, you bought out the entire supply at the party store, and still needed to buy more at the fish store. You might say "The eels that I bought at the party store were way more exciting than the others." The phrase "that I bought at the party store" is *restrictive* material: it takes the whole bunch of eels and restricts it so that you're only discussing a subset. It isn't bonus material; it's completely necessary, and therefore is not set off with commas.

One important related issue is that the word *that* tends to signal *restrictive* material, whereas *which* tends to signal *nonrestrictive* material. Therefore, you may have heard something like "always put a comma before which," because that's how this often goes. The situation, however, is actually a bit more complex than this rule implies, so it's better to think less in terms of *that/which*, and more in terms of *restrictive/nonrestrictive* or *bonus/necessary*.

Another source of confusion stems from the belief that a comma must be present when a conjunction is present. While commas are necessary when you are joining two independent clauses together with a conjunction, this does not mean that every conjunction must be accompanied by a comma! For instance, in the sentence, "I bought some eels at the party supply store, and drove them home," the conjunction *and* is not joining two independent clauses together. Instead, it is part of a list of actions that the subject of the sentence is accomplishing. Therefore, the sentence should be: "I bought some eels at the party supply store and drove them home."

Unclear:

1. The eels, that I bought at the party supply store, were crazy about disco music.

2. These deep sea creatures like roller derbies and, showing off incredible moves on the dance floor.

3. People, hoping for a wild night, will not be disappointed!

Clearer:

1a. The eels that I bought at the party supply store were crazy about disco music.
    or
1b. The eels, which I bought at multiple stores, were crazy about disco music.
    The original sentence sends mixed signals to your reader—where did I buy all these eels? Each of these edited sentences is clear and consistent about how it is meant to be read, and also employs the convention of which *with a comma,* that *without.*

 2. These deep sea creatures like roller derbies and showing off incredible moves on the dance floor.
    Here, "and" is not joining two independent clauses together. Instead, it is helping to list the things (roller derbies, showing off incredible moves on the dance floor) that these deep sea creatures like. Therefore, it does not require a comma.

 3. People hoping for a wild night will not be disappointed!
    The original sentence suggests that all people are all hoping for a wild night. Here, "hoping for a wild night" restricts the meaning of "people," which means that the sentence's meaning is much more specific; people hoping for a quiet night in with Netflix aren't included.

APPENDIX 2

Style Guide

"Correct" academic style, like "correct" English grammar and punctuation (see Appendix 1), does not exist in the way that many people imagine it. Academic style does not consist of a number of rules that one must follow. Instead, writers must make particular stylistic choices that are influenced by a number of factors, including the topic, the publication, and the audience. However, certain conventions of academic writing are widely accepted, and your ability to build a strong *ethos* as an author depends on your ability to understand and employ these conventions skillfully.

One way to become familiar with the conventions of academic style is to read a wide range of well-written articles and papers, carefully observing how the authors present information and persuade their readers. Though nothing can replace that kind of familiarity, this chapter will try to address some of the academic conventions that prove especially challenging or confusing for students. Our aim in presenting this chapter is to provide you with some of the building blocks of academic style, so that you can use these blocks as a foundation for a more extensive and ongoing writing education.

The Use of the First and Second Person

Students are frequently unsure whether it is acceptable to use the first or second person voice in an academic paper. In other words, they are confused about whether it's appropriate for an academic writer to make "I-statements" such as "I think," "I believe," or refer to a larger "we" community in asides such as: "surely we would all agree..." They also wonder whether it's appropriate for an academic writer to speak directly to the audience by writing, for example: "You would have to agree that," or "If you think about it, you'll see..."

There is no easy solution to these uncertainties. Academic convention permits a certain amount of flexibility in voice. The second person voice (direct address to "you") is exceedingly rare in academic writing, and will most often strike your reader as overly informal. References to the writer and the reader as part of a community ("we" or "us") are also likely to jar the readers, who may or may not consider themselves to part of the author's community. However, a limited and careful use of the first-person singular voice ("I") is acceptable and even standard, so long as it does not distract from your argument by drawing too much attention to your role as speaker. Academic writers may sometimes refer to their own research processes or to experiences that inspired their work in the first place as long as the writing remains focused ideas, claims, and evidence.

(In reading the paragraph above, you will likely have noticed that this textbook—while academic—does not 'follow the rules'. We refer to ourselves, we directly address you, etc. This is a conscious choice that we have made as writers who are very aware of who we're writing for, and why. We hope that it demonstrates the ways that stylistic decisions are led by considerations of purpose and audience: just as we write differently here than in our formal, published work, you will probably write differently in your formal Analytical Research Paper than in your more informal Symposium Presentation.)

Here are some examples of inappropriate and appropriate situations in which to use the first and second person:

Inappropriate:

We have all, at some point, argued with another person about whether an animal is cute or not.
The use of the plural first person strikes an informal tone that may not be appropriate for an academic paper, and it makes assumptions about the relationship between the writer and reader that may not be true.

I'm sure you would agree that many aspects of the Internet cat fame industry are problematic.
The inclusion of a personal conviction—"I'm sure"—and the direct address to the reader—"you"—seems too informal and presumes too much about the audience.

You know how it is: you sit down to work, and before you know it you are watching a cat video on the Internet.
This is an extremely informal use of the second person!

While Septimus (2008) contends that cat videos cause a decrease in worker productivity, I know that I often find that I am more productive after I have watched a few of these videos.
Here the insistence on personal experience as evidence seems intrusive; a reference to another secondary source or to primary evidence would be more appropriate.

Appropriate:

While cephalopods such as squids and octopodes are less conventionally "cute" than puppies and kittens, I would argue that their bubbly personalities render them equally desirable as pets.
This is an example of a non-intrusive first person voice that serves simply to introduce an idea.

Pratchett (2007) contends that large-eyed animals are objectively more adorable than those with small eyes; however, as I have previously established, his failure to consider the cuteness of whales renders his research inherently problematic. *("I" here refers to the author of the paper, but does not draw the reader's attention away from the paper.)*

The Passive Voice

One of the most frequently criticized and least frequently understood aspects of style is use of the passive voice. In order to understand the passive voice, it's helpful to think about clauses or sentences as having an *agent*, an *action*, and a *patient*. The agent is the thing or person that performs the action on the patient. For instance, in the sentence "The doctor cured a patient," the doctor is the agent, the patient is literally a patient, and the action is the curing.

"The doctor cured a patient" is a sentence where the verb is in the active voice. However, it's also possible to paraphrase this sentence so that the verb is in the passive voice. In that case, the sentence would be: "A patient was cured by the doctor." Here, the agent, the action, and the patient are exactly the same: the doctor is the agent, the patient is still a patient, and the action is still curing. What has changed here is that the patient is now the subject of the sentence. In other words, the subject of the sentence is not the thing or person *doing* the acting, but the thing or person to which the action is *being done*.

The reason why critics argue that the passive voice should be avoided in academic writing is that it can sometimes allow the author to hide or leave out the agent involved in the clause. For instance, it is perfectly correct to write the sentence: "A patient was cured." This sentence is grammatically complete, but it does not tell the reader who cured the patient. There are situations in which this would be important information for the author to give, and situations in which withholding this information could be seen as manipulative or deceitful.

You might be surprised to realize that you yourself almost certainly use the passive voice in ways that leave the agent out of a clause. When you state that a certain fact "is known" or "is accepted," you are leaving out the agent. By whom is that fact known? By whom is it accepted? By leaving out these details, you are providing an incomplete picture for your reader.

The problem with the passive voice, therefore, is not actually a problem with the passive voice at all—it's a problem with the way that authors use the passive voice to avoid providing information, either purposefully or inadvertently. By staying conscious of your own use of the passive voice, you can ensure that you do not fall into this trap.

Inappropriate:

It is widely agreed that guinea pigs make excellent, low-maintenance "starter pets" for children.
Who has agreed that this is the case? This point is central to the sentence!

The consumption of guinea pigs in regions of South America is often compared to the consumption of dogs, whales, or squirrels in other parts of the world.
By whom is this often compared?

In the nineteenth century, it was decided that guinea pigs made more attractive household pets than they did household dinners.
By whom was it decided?

Appropriate:

In the nineteenth century, pet fanciers subjected the guinea pig to every kind of indignity commonly visited upon particularly pampered pets.
The actors and their actions are clearly identified.

For example, Sir Charles Lamb of Beauport Park built an entire guinea pig city, which was called Winnipeg, and at the center of which stood a castellated hutch known as "Guinea Pig Castle."
Responsibility for building the guinea pig city is evident. Interestingly, the dependent clause "which was called Winnipeg" is written in the passive voice, but the reader can reasonably assume that it was Lamb himself who came up with the name.

Lamb wrote an elaborate fictional chronicle of the lives of his pets, in which guinea pigs were depicted as bold warriors with noble titles and ancient feuds.
Since we know that Lamb wrote the chronicle, the reader can assume that it was Lamb who depicted the guinea pigs thus.

Historian's note: All of this is true! (See: Anstruther, Ian. The Knight and the Umbrella: An Account of the Eglinton Tournament 1839.)

Thesaurus Language

One reason that inexperienced writers are drawn to the passive voice is that they mistakenly believe it to sound more "academic." Another temptation for students is to try to make their writing sound more sophisticated by using fancy synonyms for ordinary words. Students may feel especially drawn to do so after reading published scholarly articles, which often use specialized language that refers to particular concepts in their fields, but which appears to be merely fancy or highfalutin to the outside reader.

When students use a thesaurus to search for appropriately large and foreign synonyms, they are especially likely to misuse these words, as they may not know the words' exact meaning or conventional usage; while synonyms are broadly equivalent, they have different shades of meaning. Even if their use of the words is technically correct, the effect is often to produce sentences that are clumsy, unwieldy, and give the impression of trying too hard to impress the reader. More complicated does not always mean better! If you feel uncomfortable with the words that you are using to write your sentences, it is likely that this discomfort will communicate itself to the reader. There is no reason that you cannot use ordinary language to communicate sophisticated ideas—and, in fact, your reader may thank you for this choice!

Here are some examples of sentences that have been rendered unwieldy by convoluted language—and some easier-to-read versions of the same sentences.

Inappropriate:

The emotional lability of even the entirely winsome, downy-topped mammal is evidenced through the creature's aptitude for modifying its vocal emissions from plaintive to rapturous.

The customary bestowal of the infant canine at the occasion of Christmas festivals wanes now from the incomprehensible prevalence of its previous embrace.

Familial units now tend towards judging the oversight of small mammals to proffer advantageous preliminaries in the area of self-governance and constraint to their offspring.

Appropriate:

Even the cutest, furriest animals can be moody; for instance, they can go from whining or crying to barking and meowing ecstatically.

The traditional gift of a puppy at Christmas is no longer as popular as it once was.

Families now tend to view caring for pets as a task that offers valuable training in personal responsibility to their children.

The Language of Opinion

With rare exceptions, conventional academic writing emphasizes the argument that is being made rather than the author who is making that argument. This is one of the reasons for using the first person "I" exceedingly rarely, as mentioned in the first section of this style guide. We have also already discussed how and why to avoid making statements of personal opinion that highlight the author's experience rather than the argument. However, it is also important to be aware of language that implies or expresses a personal feeling or opinion about what is being discussed. This type of language is likely to be experienced by the reader as inappropriate or intrusive.

In general, words that seem to describe something positively or negatively are not appropriate in academic writing. This includes outright judgments such as "good," "bad," "wonderful," "horrible," "excellent," and "awful," but also words that are generally associated with positive or negative traits. For instance, words like "exciting," "charming," and "elegant" tend to be used when discussing positive traits, while words like "ignorant," "childish," or "dull" tend to be used when discussing negative traits.

Staying conscious of your word usage means that you can spot this type of language and replace it with language that is more neutral and more appropriate.

Here are some examples of inappropriate and appropriate language:

Inappropriate:

This commercial does a wonderful job of enchanting the viewer with its heartwarming images of animals.

Wonderful," "enchanting," and "heartwarming" are words that have strong positive connotations.

In its outrageous and humorous new advertising campaign, Pets Or Bust stages animal fashion shows in which puppies and kittens model the brand's stylish pet costumes.

"Outrageous" and "humorous" are opinions. "Stylish" is also an opinion, unless it refers only to the particular "make" of costume.

A recent article in *Pets Monthly* paints a devastating picture of a possible future in which, depressingly, people no longer dress their pets in outfits for holidays and parades.

"Devastating" and "depressingly" are opinions.

Appropriate:

This commercial aims to enchant viewers with the images of animals.

Here, the same idea as in the sentence above has been expressed without implying opinions.

In its new advertising campaign, Pets Or Bust stages animal fashion shows in which puppies and kittens model the brand's pet costumes.

The opinion words in the previous sentence were not actually contributing to the sentence's meaning, and can be removed.

A recent article in *Pets Monthly* paints a picture of a possible future in which people no longer dress their pets in outfits for holidays and parades—a future that some pet owners might find devastating.

This sentence no longer focuses on the author's personal opinion, but instead offers a neutral observation.

Referring to Experts

In Chapter 5, we offered some practical tips on integrating secondary sources into your work. However, the skillful introduction and contextualization of secondary sources and their authors is primarily an issue of style. Writers must learn not only which and how much information to provide about secondary sources, but also how to communicate this information in a way that feels natural and unforced.

A few basic rules of thumb exist in this area: It is a stylistic convention to refer to experts by their full names when mentioning them for the first time, then thereafter by their last names only. ("Elizabeth Inchbald writes... Inchbald considers that...") However, certain experts may be so widely known that it is not always necessary to introduce them by their full names. For instance, Freud is so famous as the founder of psychoanalysis that it might only be necessary to refer to him as "Sigmund Freud" if you are also referring to another expert whose last name is Freud—perhaps Sigmund's daughter, Anna Freud—and do not want your reader to become confused.

When introducing experts, it is also conventional to indicate to your reader why this particular expert is relevant to the discussion or argument. This is not the same as providing a list of the expert's credentials! Your goal is simply to give the reader some brief context that establishes this expert's credibility. For example, a writer whose paper concerns Gothic novels would introduce an expert as "Gothic novel enthusiast Catherine Morland" rather than "Catherine Morland, who is a Gothic novel enthusiast, holds an MA in anthropology from Oxford University, and works in the Rare Books and Manuscripts Library at The Ohio State University." At the same time, a writer whose paper concerns the treatment of rare books might introduce the same expert as "Catherine Morland of The Ohio State University's Rare Books and Manuscripts Library," since that is more relevant than her enthusiasm for Gothic novels.

When you are discussing a particular article or book, you may find it relevant to include the year in which this text was published. However, as when introducing an expert, you should not include more information than is relevant. For instance, it is appropriate to write, "In 'Problematic Effects of the Gothic Novel in British Society' (1994), Morland comments on the growing embrace of Gothic novels; however, by the early twenty-first century, other social historians had observed a different trend." It would not be appropriate to write, "In her article 'Problematic Effects of the Gothic Novel in British Society,' published in 1994 in *Gothic Novel Quarterly*, a peer-reviewed academic journal published by The Ohio State University...." In this case, you are providing far too much information, which could even cause your reader to doubt the source's credibility.

Here are some further examples of appropriate and inappropriate references to experts:

Inappropriate:

Love of pets is often commented upon by those who wish to improve a person's reputation. Peter McPhee, the accomplished Australian academic and former provost of the University of Melbourne, who holds a PhD in history, describes in his book *Robespierre: A Revolutionary Life*, published in 2012 by Yale University Press, how the French Revolutionary dictator Maximilien Robespierre used to frolic on the Champs-Élysées with his faithful dog Brount.

This is far more information than the casual reader needs.

The British author Hilary Mantel, who has won the Man Booker Prize twice and holds a law degree, depicts sixteenth-century statesman Thomas Cromwell as fond of kittens in her novel *Wolf Hall*, which was published in 2009, won many prizes, and was made into a television show.
The information that Mantel holds a law degree does not seem relevant to this sentence.

"It's true that a love of pets makes people seem kinder," writes Dr. H.U. Lofting, who is a Professor of History at The Ohio State University and has published two books on the roles of animals in history, both through Yale University Press. "Animals have become propaganda tools, albeit very cute ones."
The name of the press that has published these books does not seem relevant, and you may also consider trimming the amount of information you offer about Lofting's specialty.

Appropriate:

Love of pets is often commented upon by those who wish to improve a person's reputation. In his 2012 biography of Robespierre, historian Peter McPhee describes how the French Revolutionary dictator Maximilien Robespierre used to frolic on the Champs-Élysées with his faithful dog Brount.
Here, the paragraph concisely tells the reader that McPhee has written a biography of Robespierre—establishing why he is being referenced.

British novelist Hilary Mantel, in her award-winning fictional account of the life of Thomas Cromwell, *Wolf Hall*, depicts the sixteenth-century politician as fond of kittens.
This sentence briefly tells the reader that Mantel is an award-winning novelist who has written about Cromwell.

"It's true that a love of pets makes people seem kinder," writes animal historian H.U. Lofting. "Animals have become propaganda tools, albeit very cute ones."
The key information here is that Lofting is an animal historian—which this sentence tells the reader.

INDEX

Abstractions, 111, 113
Academic discourse, 2
Active verbs in revising thesis
    statement, 91–92
American Dialect Society, 137
Analogy, 82
Analysis, 25–26, 31–54. *See also*
    Rhetorical analysis
  art of, overview, 31–32
  drawing out implications, 41–45
  explicit meanings or messages, 25
  implicit messages and meanings,
    25–26
  observation and interpretation
    strategies, 37–41
  overview, 25–26, 31–32
  patterns of repetition, contrast,
    and anomalies, 45–51 (*See also*
    The Method)
  personal associations and, 54
  purpose of, 25
  step-by-step strategy for
    approaching, 32, 37–54 (*See
    also* Five Analytical Moves
    (from *Writing Analytically*))
  walls, 31–32
  windows, 33–36
Analysis and Personal Associations
    (from *Writing Analytically*), 54
Analytical Research Paper, 5–6
Analytical Research Project (ARP), 3–6
  Analytical Research Paper, 5–6
  Annotated Bibliography, 5
  ethos, logos, and *pathos* in, 24
  goal, 3
  MLA citation format, 6, 16
  overview, 3
  Primary Source Analysis, 5
  primary sources, 3–4
  Research Conference, 5
  Secondary Source Integration, 5
  secondary sources, 4–5
  steps of, 5–6
Annotated Bibliography, 5
Anomalies
  looking for patterns of, in The
    Method, 45–46, 49, 50, 51

in summary and analysis of
    Whistler's Mother, 53
Anticlimax, 126
"Anything Goes" School of
    Interpretation, 80
Apostrophes, possessive, 132–133
Apple computer advertisement, 34,
    36, 56–57, 87
Argument
  circular, 67–68
  contributions of secondary
    sources to, 59
  images for expansion of, 113
  paraphrasing, 60
*Arrangement In Grey and Black: The
    Artist's Mother* (Whistler),
    51–54, 76
Ars Rhetorica (Aristotle), 22
Asking "so what?," 41–45
  in a chain, 43–45
Assumptions, 32
The Atlantic, 58
Audience
  introduction for, 115
  in rhetorical analysis, 26–27
  rhetoric to persuade, 21–22, 65
    (*See also* Means of persuasion)
  secondary sources to persuade,
    59, 60
  for Symposium Presentation, 6
  active listening response, 7
  Symposium Script to
    educate, 7
Austen, Jane, 137
Author
  in copyrighted image, citation
    format for, 17
  in rhetorical situation, 22
The A.V. Club, 58
Avoiding the Extremes: Neither
    "Fortune Cookie" nor
    "Anything Goes" (from
    Writing Analytically), 79–80
  "Anything Goes" School of
    Interpretation, 80
  Fortune Cookie School of
    Interpretation, 79–80

Ballenger, Bruce, 88
Barbie dolls, 78
Beginning, starting at, 34
"Beyond Almonds: A Rogue's
    Gallery of Guzzlers in
    California's Drought" (Charles
    for NPR), 29–30
Biases of secondary sources, 58
Binary oppositions, 45, 46, 47, 49,
    50, 60
Bird by Bird (Lamott), 40
Blade Runner, 57
Body paragraphs, 120–122
    development of, 120
    drafting research paper as series
        of, 121
    idea of, 120–121
    length of, 121–122
    linking sentences in, 122
    unity of, 120
Burtynsky, Edward, 44
BY: Attribution (CC license
    specification), 15

Charles, D., 29
Circular argument, 67–68
Citations
    acknowledging sources in
        text, 61
    format for images, 16–20
        Creative Commons, 18–19
        fair use of copyrighted image,
            17–18
        original work, 19
        public domain, 19
    of sources after quotations, 62
Claims
    evidence distinguished from,
        68–69
    labeling sentences as, 68
    qualifying, 71
    in rhetoric, 27, 28–30
    unsubstantiated, 67–68
    in weak thesis statement
        thesis that basis its claim on
            personal conviction,
            107–108
        thesis that makes an overly
            broad claim, 108
        thesis that makes no claim, 105

Classroom participation, 8
Clauses, 128–129
Columbia University, 14
Commas, 139–141
    forbidden, 140–141
    required, 139–140
Comma splices, 131–132
Composition *vs.* writing, 11–12
Conclusion, 124–126
    function of, 124
    movements (culmination and
        send-off), 124–125
    observation pushing to, 43
    problems in, 125–126
        anticlimax, 126
        overstatement, 126
        raising a totally new point,
            125
        redundancy, 125
Context
    interpretive, 74–79
    in rhetoric, 27, 28–30
Context and the Making of Meaning
    (from *Writing Analytically*),
    75–79
    Intention as an Interpretive
        Context, 77–78
    Specifying an Interpretive
        Context: A Brief Example,
        76–77
    What Is and Isn't "Meant" to Be
        Analyzed, 78–79
Contradictions, 60, 111–113
Contrast
    looking for patterns of, in The
        Method, 45–51
    in summary and analysis of
        Whistler's Mother, 53
Conventional wisdom, 106–107
Copyright, 12–17
    Creative Commons, 14–15,
        18–19
    defined, 12
    fair use
        of copyrighted image,
            17–18
        of copyrighted materials,
            12–14
    original works, 16
    public domain images, 16

Redundancy
  in conclusions, 125
  in transitions, 123
Referring to experts, 148–150
Repetition
  in conclusions, 125
  development and, 93
  of key words, 122
  of key works in body paragraphs,
    122
  looking for patterns of, in The
    Method, 45–51
  raising a totally new point to
    avoid, 125
  in summary and analysis of
    Whistler's Mother, 53
  in transitions, 123
  in weak thesis statement, 92–93
Required commas, 139–140
Research Conference, 5
Research paper, 65–85
  body paragraphs, 120–122
  conclusion, 124–126
  evidence in, 66–71 (See also
    Linking Evidence and Claims
    (from Writing Analytically))
  form of, 115–126
    body paragraphs, 120–122
    conclusion, 124–126
    introduction, 115–119
    transitions, 122–123
  goal of, 65
  introduction, 115–119
  rhetorical choices in writing, 65
  substance of, 65–66
  transitions, 122–123
"Revealing" as trigger for analysis,
    38–39
Rhetoric
  Aristotle's guide to, 22
  defined, 21–22
  ethos, 22–23
  explicit meanings or messages, 25
  implicit messages and meanings,
    25–26
  investigating (See Rhetorical
    analysis)
  logos, 22, 23
  pathos, 22, 23–24
  visual, 109
  in writing research paper, 65

Rhetoric (Aristotle), 22
Rhetorical analysis, 26–30
  in Analytical Research Project, 30
  elements in, 27–28
    claim, 27
    context, 27
    current, 27–28
    examples of, 28–30
    "It just is" mistake, 27
    noticing and, 39–40
    purpose of, 26
    "they didn't mean it that way"
      mistake, 27
Rhetorical situation, 22–24
  audience in, 22
  author in, 22
  text in, 22–24
Run-on sentences, 130–131

SA: Share-alike (CC license
    specification), 15
Secondary Source Integration, 5
Secondary sources, 55–63. See also
    Citations; Quotations
  in Analytical Research Project, 4–5
  choosing, 56
  contributions of, to argument, 59
  credibility, evaluating, 57–59
  finding, 56
  how to use, 59–60
  importance of, 55–56
  overview, 55
  paraphrasing, 5, 59–60
  referring to, 148–150
  research questions, examples of,
    56–57
Second person voice, 143–145
Second pronoun, 136
Seems to Be About X, But Could Also
    Be (Or Is "Really") About Y
    (from Writing Analytically), 83–85
  doing, 83–84
  Seems to Be About X . . .: An
    Example, 84–85
Send-off, 124–125
Sentence fragments, 128–129
Sentences
  in body paragraphs, 120, 122
  in freewriting, 40
  fused (or run-on), 130–131
  incoherent, 116